Lena Wright Myers, Professor of Sociology at Jackson State University, Jackson, Mississippi, has directed numerous research projects. She has published many articles in professional journals. She is also a contributing author to *Another Voice: Feminist Perspectives on Social Life and Social Science* and *The Black Woman.*

Dr. Myers is a native of Hattiesburg, Mississippi. Her B.A. is from Tougaloo College and her M.A. and Ph.D. from Michigan State University.

In Memory of Julius Myers, Jr.,
my beloved husband
whose strengths
enhanced my ability to cope

Black Women
DO THEY COPE BETTER?

Lena Wright Myers

A SPECTRUM BOOK

Prentice-Hall, Inc., Englewood Cliffs, New Jersey 07632

Library of Congress Cataloging in Publication Data

MYERS, LENA WRIGHT.
　Black women, do they cope better?

　(A Spectrum Book)
　Bibliography: p.
　Includes index.
　　1.　Afro-American Women.　2.　Afro-Americans—
Psychology.　I.　Title.
E185.86.M97　　　　305.4'0973　　　　80-21595
ISBN　0-13-077834-6
ISBN　0-13-077826-5 (pbk.)

Editorial/production supervision by Betty Neville
Cover design by Ira Shapiro
Cover illustration by John Rowe
Manufacturing buyer: Cathie Lenard

Printed in the United States of America

10　9　8　7　6　5　4　3　2　1

Prentice-Hall International, Inc., *London*
Prentice-Hall of Australia Pty. Limited, *Sydney*
Prentice-Hall of Canada, Ltd., *Toronto*
Prentice-Hall of India Private Limited, *New Delhi*
Prentice-Hall of Japan, Inc., *Tokyo*
Prentice-Hall of Southeast Asia Pte. Ltd., *Singapore*
Whitehall Books Limited, *Wellington, New Zealand*

CONTENTS

preface *vii*

chapter one
IT'S ABOUT COPING AND SELF-ESTEEM *1*

chapter two
"BUSY TALK" ABOUT BLACK WOMEN 7

chapter three
COPING—HOW? *17*

chapter four
SOCIAL SUPPORT SYSTEMS FOR BLACK WOMEN *25*

chapter five
FEELING GOOD ABOUT ROLES *41*

chapter six
THE MYTH OF BLACK EMASCULATION *63*

chapter seven
BLACK WOMEN/BLACK MEN RELATIONSHIPS *69*

chapter eight
SELF-IMAGES OF BLACK WOMEN *85*

appendix *93*

bibliography *111*

index *117*

PREFACE

It's about coping!! It's about finding ways to deal with experiences resulting from circumstances of birth—being black and female, simultaneously. *Black Women: Do They Cope Better?* is written from the voices of 400 black women—some of whom were the heads of their families and some of whom were not, as defined by American standards. These women lived in the States of Michigan and Mississippi.

I am grateful to many persons who contributed to making this book possible. It grew out of research for my dissertation, titled "A Study of the Self-Esteem Maintenance Process Among Black Women," which was funded by the Ford Foundation in the form of a Ford Dissertation Fellowship in Ethnic Studies, 1972–73. In 1974–76, the National Science Foundation funded research for a follow-up of a related sample.

To Ruby D. Richardson, I offer thanks for having typed my initial comments while I was developing the prospectus for this book.

I am especially grateful to Dorothy Smith and Essie Rutledge, colleagues, whose insightful discussions with me about this book contributed to my success in writing the first part of the original manuscript.

I must give special recognition to Maxine S. Lyles, one of my former graduate students, who took time from her busy schedule with her profession and her daughter, Kendria, to type the manuscript.

For the mere presence of my son, Stanley Dion Myers, and his continuous moral support, which made me know the reality of the content of this book, I am extremely grateful. Of course, the book might never have been completed were it not for the encouragement of my very close support system—my parents, Alberta and Charlie Wright, and my Siblings. They all have looked forward to its completion with real enthusiasm.

To the 400 black women who provided the information for this book, I am very grateful.

My editor, Lynne Lumsden, deserves special thanks for her patience, the needed push, and the scholarly editorial comments and insight she has given me.

Thanks also go to Betty Neville for guiding the transformation of unmarked manuscript into finished book.

To all others too numerous to list in this manuscript, for your constant encouragement, I am most grateful.

IT'S ABOUT
COPING
AND
SELF-ESTEEM

Black Women: Do They Cope Better? began, mentally and emotionally, years ago. I am a black woman who was born and raised in Mississippi. I lived with both my parents within our home. During the time that I was in junior high school, I knew that many of my schoolmates were from families with one parent—their mother only. After finishing college, I began teaching in Mississippi. There, again, many of my students were products of a one-parent—the mother—family. I later went away to do doctoral studies with a strong commitment to reviewing the literature on black families in an effort toward doing research on black women who were the heads of their families. As I reviewed the literature, I became disgusted with it because of its heavy emphasis on the negative self-images of black women who headed families. Most of the available literature—originating in ignorance and bigotry— perpetuates the idea that being black, female, and head of the family in the United States is bad. Instability, illegitimacy, and being motherheaded were typically viewed as the major weaknesses of the black family. The literature strongly suggested that black women who headed their families could not possibly think well of themselves because of these weaknesses. After I completed my work, I knew that too much emphasis had been directed toward the negative aspects of the mother-headed family, with a complete neglect of certain strengths that exist among black women in this situation.

I then began pondering the following broad, intriguing questions suggested by the literature:

1. How does the black woman see her role as head of her family?
2. What does the black woman think of herself as a result of being head of her family?
3. Does being head of her family stop the black woman from having a sense of self-worth or, rather, from feeling good about herself?

I was compelled to find answers to these questions. Research on black-female family heads and the ways in which they cope with a racist and sexist society was needed. I felt that maybe doing what she has to do for the good of those close to her (her family) aids the black woman in feeling good about herself. I also wondered *who* we think of when deciding how effectively we have performed our roles as mothers, wives, providers, or whatever part we are playing. Maybe when we, as black women, compare ourselves to one another instead of being compared to middle-class white women, we think better about ourselves than the literature suggests. Because we have and are still facing similar situations, we are likely to have similar problems and needs that require defining in our own terms. Thus, we tend to develop similar ways for dealing with the pressures of racism and sexism, or, rather, for being black and female in a white, male-oriented society. Sometime later, I knew that I could no longer think of these questions without seeking answers to them. I knew that to go and talk face to face with black women about their ways of coping with the pressures of a confused, racist, and sexist society was a necessary goal. I did just that. I talked to 400 black women—200 from Grand Rapids, Michigan, in 1972 and 200 from Jackson, Mississippi, in 1974. I interviewed these women in order to compare black women who were the heads of their families with black women who had male mates who were assumed to be the family heads by the larger society. These were women who (1) had lived with their spouses for five years or more and (2) women who were divorced, separated, or widowed. They were 20 to 81 years old. They had educations that ranged from the third grade to master's degrees and above. These women had from one to fifteen children and *monthly family* incomes of from $60 to $2500. They had lived in Grand Rapids, Michigan, or Jackson, Mississippi, for from one to eighty-one years. Three hundred and three of the black women had been married only once, and ninety-seven had been married at least twice. One hundred and seventy-one worked full time. There were ninety-two who were married and worked and seventy-nine who were without a male mate and worked.

What the black women told me is unique in that it focuses upon how these women develop and maintain a good image of themselves. Yet it builds upon previous works not hampered by faulty white models (Bernard 1966; Billingsley 1968; Hill 1971; Jackson 1972; Ladner 1971; Reid 1972; Staples 1970).

One year and nine months ago, and well after this book was begun, I had to reexamine my own coping mechanisms for dealing with a tragic situation of which I had a great deal of social psychological knowledge—but no firsthand experience. After several years of marriage, I too became the head of my family as a result of the sudden death of my husband. My son and my work became my coping mechanisms more intensely than ever.

There are two concepts that are critical to understanding this book. They are *self-esteem* and *coping*. I define coping as alternative ways of dealing with the pressures of society. Hence coping helps to provide some explanation of resources used by black women in adjusting to the various social pressures they experience in everyday life. This is to say that there is a *causal* relationship between what the black woman thinks of herself, and coping. It is to suggest that feelings of self-worth lead to a greater ability to cope.

"BUSY TALK" ABOUT BLACK WOMEN*

Black women carry the dual stigma of being female and black in a society that devalues both. The ways in which we are seen in social research generally support this devaluing. Much has been written about black women based on personal generalizations or on what someone else feels our experiences have been. The "laboring in the field" concept of slavery, which is credited for creating a so-called black matriarchy, has been used almost to its fullest. Census data since 1960 showed that nearly one-fourth of all black families in the United States were headed by a woman. Many writers, researchers, and public policymakers have since misinterpreted these figures. Such misleading terms

8

as *unstable, inadequate, broken home,* and *ineffective* are often used to describe the black-female-headed family. The meanings of such terms are actually dependent upon the "eyes of the beholder." And this is what I call "busy talk." Busy talk with little substance.

First, scholars assume that as blacks measuring ourselves against whites, we—as black women—should have little chance for feeling good about ourselves. If one looks at the location of blacks in various institutional structures and at the numerous disadvantages we face, it would not be hard to conclude, as many have done, that black women have low self-images. Finding little comfort for black women as women, much criticism has been directed toward the mother-headed family as a perpetuator of the disadvantaged situation of black people in general. But the problem lies in the fact that the least desired family structure in North America seems to be the mother-headed structure, and that black mothers are often "blamed"— directly or indirectly—for the problem of black poverty (Myers 1975).

Under such conditions then, much of the traditional sociological and pyschological literature—for example, *The Moynihan Report and the Politics of Controversy,* edited by Rainwater and Yancey; the works of Karon (1958), and others—have concluded that black women could not possibly value themselves. One *very* dominant view of black-women family heads is that of *The Moynihan Report and the Politics of Controversy,* which concludes that nearly a quarter of married black women are divorced or separated, that 35 percent of all black children live in broken homes, that almost a quarter of black births are illegitimate, and that nearly one-fourth of all black families are headed by women. Moynihan suggests that although these figures show a smaller proportion of the black community in trouble than is often claimed, the figures are not totally representative of the extent of the problem. Tracing the fundamental causes of the matriarchally structured family to slavery and unemployment, Moynihan suggested that the system has directed the black woman into a position of economic and familial dominance, which she has maintained—willingly or not—until the present day.

Powdermaker (1939), Burgess and Locke (1945), and Karon (1958:32) also viewed the matriarchally structured family as having derived from slavery. According to Powdermaker:

> Under slavery the mother remained the important figure in the family. The affectional relations of mother and child developed deep and permanent attachment. Frequently, also, the father was a member of the family group, but often the relationship was casual and easily broken. . . . Then, too, Negro husbands were sold more often. These and other factors contributed to the development of a matricentric form of the family during slavery. (1939)

Given the historical roots of the black family, Pettigrew (1964) proposes that both poverty and migration have acted to maintain the old slave pattern of a mother-centered family today. According to Pettigrew, not only does desperate poverty disturb healthy family life through dilapidated housing, crowded living conditions, restricted recreational facilities, and direct contact with the most corrupting elements of urban disorganization; but it also makes the ideal

American pattern of household economics practically impossible. He also suggests that employment discrimination has made it more difficult for poorly educated black men to secure steady employment than for poorly educated black women to do so. When the unskilled black man does manage to secure a job, he generally assumes an occupation that pays barely enough to support himself—much less a family. These conditions obviously limit the ability of the lower-class black to follow the typical American pattern—that is, a stable unit, with the husband providing a steady income for his family.

We learn who we are and what we are by carefully observing how other people react to us, and according to Pettigrew, this process is highly structured for blacks by the roles they are expected to play. When a black man attempts to gain an image of himself on the basis of his typical contacts with white America, he receives primarily negative responses. Kardiner and Ovesey (1951) similarly propose conscious and unconscious trends among blacks toward "self-hatred and identification with whites." As Banks and Grambs summarized:

> For the Black . . . in white American society, the generalized other whose attitudes he assumes and the looking glass into which he gazes both reflect the same judgment; he is inferior because he is Black. His self-image, developed in the lowest stratum of a color caste system, is shaped, defined, and evaluated by a generalized other which is racist or warped by racists. (Banks and Grambs 1972:56)

If the black man is seen as the primary victim, in this

view, the black woman may be in part a villain. Pettigrew sees black women as contributing to the general cultural put-down of black men:

> The Negro wife in this situation can easily become disgusted with her financially dependent husband, and her rejection of him further alienates the male from family life. Embittered by their experiences with men, many Negro mothers often act to perpetuate the mother-centered pattern by taking a greater interest in their daughters than their sons. For example, more Negro females graduate from college than Negro males, the reverse of the pattern found among white Americans. (Pettigrew 1964:16)

Other reports similarly identify the problems of blacks with black women as mothers and household heads. Kardiner and Ovesey conclude in their study that the black mother participates in a cycle of poor mothering, passed on from generation to generation.

> In discussing the broken home as one of the expressions of the Negro personality, we seem to commit the error of using it both as a cause and as an effect. This is not an error. It is the kind of cycle that is easily demonstrable in any culture. . . . With maternal neglect, we can trace the effects of this in the individual so that when the child becomes a mother she then repeats the same thing; she neglects and rejects her children. This is not an imitative process by any means; it is the end result of an integrative process. (Kardiner and Ovesey 1951:344)

Kardiner and Ovesey also assume that the maternal-household situation takes a heavy toll on opportunities for developing strong affective ties. First, the needs for dependence are frustrated, making the mother a frustrating object, rather than one the child can depend on. However, as suggested by these authors, this does not mean that it is the intention of the mothers to neglect or mistreat their children. In the words of these authors, "quite the contrary, the intention is the usual one, and many lower-class Negro mothers have strong maternal feelings, are exceedingly protective, and try to be good providers." The researchers' findings showed frustration and arbitrary discipline on the part of mothers who were heads of their households.

Black women, moreover, have their own identity problems to cope with, according to dominant social science views. Grier and Cobbs (1968) discuss the condition of the black woman within her own community as one that is perplexingly involved with her historic relationship to white society—a society that has defined and structured that relationship for her. They describe differences of experiences of black and of white women, and suggest that an awareness of these differences will illuminate the nature of the black woman's identity crisis.

> The first measure of a child's worth is made by her mother, and if, as is the case with so many Black people in America, the mother feels that she herself is a creature of little worth, this daughter, however valued and desired, represents her scorned self. Thus the girl can be loved and valued only within a limited sphere, and can never be the flawless child, because she is who she is—Black and inevitably linked to her Black, depreciated mother—always seen to be lacking, deficient, and faulty in some way. (1968:40)

They conclude that neither the family nor the community at large can undo this attitude of the black woman toward the "self" because of the fact that she is black.

In addition to social psychological issues, researchers acknowledge the difficult nature of the social tasks faced by black mothers. Rainwater, for example, proposes that whether the black mother is working or on welfare, she still has the problem of maintaining a household, socializing her children, and achieving for herself some sense of membership in relation to other women and men. According to Rainwater, she knows that it is a hard, hopeless, and often thankless task to serve as head of household, but she also knows that it is at least possible (Rainwater, in Parsons and Clark 1966:160-200).

Of course it's possible! In some instances, mother-headed families are so common that they may be fostering a much more positive image of such families than traditional social scientists might assume.

Since black-women-headed families are common, they may not *necessarily* be viewed as unstable or broken family forms by black women. Before interviewing the women for this book, it was assumed that women who did not work and who had one or more children to support did not think as well of themselves as working women heads and nonheads of families or married women who did not work. However, I found that this is not true. The unemployed women heads of families in Mississippi thought as well of themselves as all the rest of the women I talked to.

It appears that they (the social scientists) may not be the unequivocal experts at all. Unless one is black and female, it is almost impossible to do enough valid research and offer enough sophisticated statistics to give a fair view of the dilemma of black women in a white, male-oriented society. Thus we find ourselves with concepts that are totally erroneous. Of course, it might be nice—although less fascinating—if simple answers to the "hows" and "whys" of the behavior of black women could suffice.

I argue that it is time for a new view of black women, one that allows for the possibility of self-esteem and pride. Blacks do not necessarily measure themselves against whites; nor do black women measure themselves against white women. Sure, the mother-headed family has some weaknesses as well as some strengths, as do all other types of families. But let us realize that being the mother head of a family may be the source of strength and pride for black women. As one scholar puts it:

> No other woman on earth could have emerged from the hell of force and temptation which once engulfed and still surrounds Black women in America with half the modesty and womanliness they retain. (DuBois 1969:186)

COPING—
HOW?

Have you ever asked yourself, "How well do I cope?" Or rather, "What do I do to get through a hard day?" Scarcely does a day go by in which the demand to meet the "hustle and bustle" of the real world is not present. Emergencies, accidents, incompetencies, the failure of people all around us, and circumstances beyond our control—all may go against our planned activities. But what do we do?

Do you consider kicking the dog, biting your nails, or pulling out your eyelashes (the latter two are examples of what therapists may call "nervous tics") ways of coping with stressful situations? Or are you a bored housewife who abuses alcohol as an escape mechanism when you are left

18

alone for long periods of time while your top-executive, highly salaried husband travels from coast to coast on business trips? Does the use of tranquilizers (maybe Valium) make tomorrow look brighter to you even though "tomorrow is tomorrow" and not today? Do you simply wallow in self-pity, or do you panic on a long-term basis because your husband or mate has left you with four children aged 2 to 8 to raise? When asked, "Are you married?" are you reluctant to say that you are divorced, separated, or even widowed— because society says that the ideal type of family structure is one where both parents are in the home raising their children? Or do you sit idly hoping that today's stressful or unpleasant experiences will not come with tomorrow? What are some of the things you do to head off the "letdown" that comes when you are confronted with adverse experiences? If you have not already done it, I am suggesting that you begin to think about these questions. Maybe none of these examples fit you. But I assure you that you use or, rather, do something as a way of coping with life situations—successfully or unsuccessfully.

As a sociologist, I have made several observations about how people cope, specifically black-women heads of families. Before talking to the 400 women for my research, I had some feeling for how we cope with the emotional degradation we have experienced. It was my belief that our key to coping with racism and sexism, as black women, was to get an image of ourselves based on how well we do whatever we are doing, and on how others whose opinions matter to us view our successes in whatever we are doing. Since talking with the black women, I am now convinced of this.

Yet some writers hold onto the notion that we, as blacks, have difficulties in deciding who we are. According to one writer:

> The quest for self-identity is the search for answers to the all important questions: Who am I? What am I as a person? And how do I fit into the world? These are not easy questions for anyone to answer in our complex, swiftly moving society. Yet, they offer even greater difficulties for Negro Americans. (Pettigrew 1964:7)

But why? Why must it be assumed that we necessarily have to get our images of ourselves through our contacts with white Americans, when we have each other (blacks) with whom to identify? Remember the old cliché—"People are judged by the company they keep"? Maybe some people are not looking at the company some of us keep!! If we accept that cliché as truth, then for the most part, black women are often in the company of other black women. That being the case, simple deductive reasoning would indicate that black women should be judged, if at all, in accordance with other black women, not with their white counterparts. Still accepting that cliché as truth would lead to the conclusion that not only do black women choose other black women as the company they keep; they also may very well do so because they do not want to identify with white women, as so many social scientists suggest. In addition, segregation in every aspect of American life saw to it that we were together by necessity for a number of years. But people who face similar situations are likely to have similar problems to cope with. Our situations are similar because we face similar or common physical and social environments. Of course, as black women, our common physical and social environments are realistic and many. We are more than just the heads of our families, laden down with the negative consequences that Euro-Americans say should go along with taking that role. More? Yes!!! As some literature suggests: We are college graduates, dropouts, students, wives, mothers, lovers, children of the ghetto, products of the bourgeoisie, professional writers, people who never dreamed of publishing, members of the movement, gentle humanists, violent revolutionaries, angry and tender, loving and hating. We are all of these things and more. Sure we are! It may not be so obvious, but it is equally true that as black women, separated in space but belonging to the same social category (race, sex, and, in some cases, age) we have come to recognize our common fate. Thus, we may deal with the effects of racism and sexism in a somewhat uniform manner (see Clark 1974:37). For example, a divorced black woman who is temporarily uncertain about several decisions she must make regarding her children may contact another divorced woman for the purpose of discussing her uncertainties. Her willingness to accept her friend's support suggests her approval and acceptance of that friend's opinions on how to solve her own problem. For the most part, this woman will be more receptive to the opinions and support of women who are themselves experiencing similar problems. Ann* is a 38-year-old divorced mother of four children who lives in Mississippi. She had no problem talking to me about what

---

*A pseudonym is used to identify the women and their husbands or former husbands for some examples since, to assure confidentiality, names of the respondents were *not* secured.

she does when problems come up. She said, "I call on Mildred (divorcee, age 42) when something comes up that I can't handle, because we go through some of the same things." She told me that they had been "close friends for years." What do Ann and Mildred have in common? They are both divorced black women with children. They are both heads of families and victims of society's negative views of their being heads of their families.

If we know who we are and what we are about, we should know fairly well how we will deal with unpleasant experiences. This simply means "tapping our inner resources." And after "tapping our inner resources," we develop an image of ourselves—either negative or positive. The majority of the black women I interviewed expressed a positive image of themselves, aspects of which are discussed later.

How do we come to think well of ourselves? Staples states:

> The functions ascribed to the female have always been important to their societies. It has usually been the custom to devalue these functions simply because they are female tasks—not because they are unimportant. But upon her arrival on the shores of the Americas, the Black woman acquired a role unique in the annals of mankind. (1973:11)

He concludes that it is this period that we must look to for an understanding of contemporary black women.

Have you ever met a person who is doing a number of different things during the course of her lifetime—for example, mothering, wifing, working, (both outside and inside the home), and so on? You probably wonder how much success she is meeting in the many things she is doing. Or is she really successful at any *one* thing? There are differences in the extent to which success in her various roles affects what she thinks of herself. We do not necessarily evaluate ourselves on the basis of any one role. Instead we may select certain roles (from a number of them) to measure our success in order to think well of ourselves, and those roles are most often *occupational* and *family maintenance*. And for the black women I talked to, working while being a mother to their children were the two most important roles. How black women view their success in performing those roles (which they have chosen from several) and how they are viewed by other black women playing similar roles serve as ways of coping with adverse experiences in their lives. This is not to imply that black women are happy or even excited over the notion of being the heads of their families. Nor am I saying that we are "superwomen" in terms of physical strength. Coping is not to be interpreted as being hardened to the effects of adversity. We certainly are vulnerable to being moved by such things as sorrow, loneliness, neglect, unhappiness, and even by happiness. But we are also capable of finding the means or, rather, the alternatives for developing and maintaining our emotional stability by feeling good about ourselves, at least some of the time, while living in a society that is not in tune with being black and or with being female—and at the same time! However, coping does mean facing up to the reality that the road back from crisis experience is always hardest at its beginning. It means taking tiny steps forward because small triumphs build confidence in ourselves. And those small triumphs are the things from which our "emotional gusto" comes—helping us to persevere through unpleasant experiences in everyday life.

SOCIAL SUPPORT
SYSTEMS
FOR BLACK WOMEN

What is a *social support system?* For this book, I define social support systems as those helping agents or individuals within their environment whom black women identify as those who provide social support and feedback in solving problems or during periods of crisis. As black women, the heads of families seek out the same groups, collectives, and individuals for support as do other black women in general. But like other groups, black-women heads of households tend to look most often to women in their own group for support because of the commonality of their circumstances. Their unique position in the family commands a specific set of social problems and also a unique set of responses. It is therefore assumed that black women who share similar experiences with respect to their status as heads of family will share similar life events and experiences, and that their responses to such experiences will also be similar in many respects. For example, the experiences of Pearl, a black cook, may be cited as typical:

> *"When I worked in Chet's Restaurant, I came to work fifteen minutes late one morning because the first bus running that morning was late. The manager (white) threatened to fire me. But the next day, Carol (white woman) was an hour late, and she said it was because her husband's car would not start. He told her, 'It's OK because we all have car trouble sometime in life.' Three weeks later, Fannie (black woman) whose little girl had the flu, called in to say that she would be late because she had to take her child to the clinic. When she showed up two hours later, the manager fired her 'on the spot.' Now . . . tell me that Fannie and I don't have some of the same problems."*

Black women know what it means to be oppressed and readily identify acts of racial discrimination. However, black women realize that there are alternatives for coping with oppression and for developing and maintaining a positive sense of self.

What social support systems are most often used by black-mother heads of families in efforts to deal with basic social, emotional, financial, or other kinds of problems? Among the various possible social networks, the ones assumed to be used most often are the following: family, friends, church, clergyman. The diagram that follows may help to explain the social support systems used.

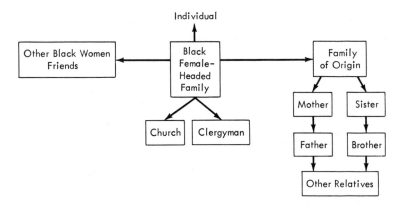

In looking at the diagram, it appears that close friends and family are of equal importance. It may even be safe to speculate that the close friends were more important to some of the black women I talked to than some family members. The women in my study stated that they felt more relaxed in talking with close, black women friends about their problems. Close friends were found to be more supportive of their emotional feelings, values, and beliefs. In society at large, members do tend to discuss some problems only with personal friends rather than with family members. This, again, is a way of coping with otherwise "unbearable" life situations.

MOTHERS/MOTHER SUBSTITUTES

How the black woman sees her parents certainly affects how she feels about herself. This is true for others as well. However, existing literature suggests that black females do not have adequate role models for what white society defines as ideal behavior, examples of which are noted in " 'Busy Talk' About Black Women" (Chapter 2). The key word here is *adequate*. What may appear to be inadequate to some people may be quite adequate to others. Adequacy, in other words, depends upon one's own definition of the term.

For the black women I talked to, their mothers or mother substitutes were their role models. Try to recall the times you have talked to a black woman about issues of everyday life—for example, raising children, women/men relationships, the cost of living, and so on. Approximately how many times did you hear her mention something about her mother or mother substitute while she was growing up? The women I interviewed saw their mothers/ mother substitutes as sources of social support in coping with life's problems. Most of them said that the *one* woman they looked up to and admired more than any other was their mother or mother substitute.

> *A 52-year-old divorcee recalled that when she, her three sisters, and two brothers were growing up, they would sometimes talk among themselves about what a "good mother" they had. She (her mother) had something that she would call "inner strength" that kept her going. The thing that made her want to be like her was that she made a way when life seemed impossible. And after she made a way for them, she acted like she felt so good about it.*

More than 68 percent of the black-female heads of families said that during their teenage years, they felt that they wanted to be like their mothers or mother substitutes when they grew up. Why did the majority feel this way? Ninety-four percent listed positive qualities in their mother-role models with which they wanted to identify. It is not likely that black women or anyone else would want to be like a person if they did not see some positive characteristics in that person to emulate. For example:

> *A 52-year-old employed mother of six children who was separated from her husband said her mother was "more than a mother—she was a friend to her too."*

> *Another unmarried woman from Mississippi said; "I had a very 'giving' mother. She gave so much love and showed warmth to her children."*

> *A clerk typist for an insurance company in Grand Rapids viewed herself like her mother in that "she never made a difference in her children. Whatever she did for one of us, she did it for the others."*

> *A 24-year-old waitress and mother of two children stated that her mother taught her cleanliness, was always clean and neat . . . really kept herself up.*

> *An unemployed divorcee and mother of three children said, "Mother had a lot of common sense. And I really liked that in her."*

> *Still another unmarried woman said, "My mother hated a liar—and I do too."*

> *A factory worker for an automobile corporation in Michigan said that she always wanted to be like her mother because "She was a terrific black woman in every sense of the word."*

A retired widow said her mother "had faith in herself and her children."

An ADC (Aid to Dependent Children) mother of three children, age 31, said: "My mother taught me what life was all about in her own way of thinking. She raised all of us without a father, so why can't I raise my children without one?"

Other reasons for wanting to be "like mother/mother substitute" included the following:

"She was a good mother, and I am too."

"She showed so much love for her children and other people's children too."

"She was such a strong woman."

"She was honest. . . . Her word was her bond."

"She was well liked by so many people."

"She had a very pleasant attitude and disposition."

"My mother was always warm and kind. Even when things were not going well with her, she managed to wear a smile and speak a kind word."

A college teacher, age 28, divorced, and mother of two, said she wanted to be like her mother because her mother had a rough time in life, but she still "made it."

And a 28-year-old woman who was separated from her husband and employed said she wanted to be like her mother because of her "strong belief in facing reality and reaching high goals."

It is interesting, though not surprising, that the black women of these samples defined their mothers in terms of being "effective," "assured," and "competent"—qualities they felt they, too, possessed. For example: The appearance of a divorced mother of six children who was an English teacher at a community college indicated that she had not permitted the hands of hard times to pinch wrinkles in her face during the 56 years she had lived. With a ray of self-confidence that even the least perceptive person could grasp, she obviously enjoyed talking about the depressing moments of her past in contrast to the successful times of her present. The third born among four children of a sharecropper in rural Mississippi, she was very convincing in her understanding of the strengths her mother possessed. She boasted:

> *"Out of all the hard times which we went through as children, Mother would never let us hang our heads low. She was a strong woman who could face any problem and never bend. . . . And I know that I am just like my mother."*

How did the mothers/mother substitutes help to prepare the women for coping in later life? The emotional/moral support given these people was very important to them. One woman reported that her mother always said that she first had to respect herself before expecting other people to do so. Another was often told, "You can be anything you want to be." Other responses included:

> *A Michigan woman who was the mother of one child and taught school said her mother wanted her and*

helped her in every way to get the education that she (her mother) could not get.

Another head of a family said: "Mother taught me to keep my chin up, and never stoop to any degrading situation in life, no matter how others try to keep me from getting ahead in life."

Still another family head said that her mother showed her and her sisters and brothers that she wanted them to "move toward higher goals" and pushed them toward that end.

One employed head of family from Mississippi stated that her mother taught her how to take care of her younger brothers and sisters when she was 14 years old. According to this woman, "That's how I learned to be a good mother to my own children."

A 27-year-old divorcee and mother of one from Mississippi said that her mother "made sure that she had nice clothes, was always clean, and never hungry." She also stated that her mother still helps her in providing the same kinds of things for her (the respondent's) child.

An employed head of household said that her mother's emotional and moral support were invaluable. Stating that her mother saw after the children for her while she worked, she added, "Mother was always there when I needed her."

Another employed family head, age 44, seemingly found solace in expressing how her mother helped her. She said: "Mother often told me that life is not always a bed of roses—but with faith in myself, I can make life worthwhile."

An unemployed woman from Mississippi expressed how her mother helped her: "She taught me to be proud of what I have and to always maintain respect for myself."

One woman said, "Mother stayed at home with us while we were young and didn't run in the streets like some mothers do." She went on to say, "Some mothers will even spend money on themselves and neglect their own children–but not my mother."

Another response was, "She was apt and pushed me to use my ability to learn in school in order to finish my education."

OTHER FAMILY MEMBERS

Stable families seem to be important in the development of self-esteem, although not all people are affected in the same way by a broken home (Rosenberg 1965). Rosenberg found that the effects of a broken home varied according to the age of the mother, whether the mother married, and religion. However, a number of researchers on black families implicitly suggest that "broken homes" are deterrents to the development of a sense of worthiness by its members (Burgess and Locke 1945; Grier and Cobbs 1968; Kardiner and Ovesey 1951; Karon 1958; Pettigrew 1964; and others). There seems to be an obsession with the concept of stability when social and behavioral scientists discuss or research the black family.

In reality, family stability is rapidly becoming an illusion. It is a vanishing phenomenon, even for white families within our society. For the only meaningful definition of family stability is that two people marry and stay married until one dies, and that the children, all conceived after marriage, live within the family household until their maturity. (Billingsley 1968:156)

Billingsley suggests that even with social changes and explosions all around us, society still seems obsessed with the notion that black families should be stable, with stability creating numerous desirable consequences. He refers to this as part of an illusion.

If a black woman is raised in a female-headed household, how likely is she to form a female-headed household in the future? Is there a relationship between what kind of families black women come from and what they think of themselves?

The majority of black women I talked with, whether heads of their families or not, were *not* from female-headed families. This itself tells us that female-headed families do not necessarily breed female-headed families. And for those instant authorities on black families who are promoting a "culture of poverty" thesis, my data refute that thesis. The "culture of poverty" thesis, offered by Oscar Lewis in 1968, suggested that conditions of poverty generate a sub-culture, or rather, a set of values and behavior patterns that are unique to the poor. It included such characteristics as a fatalistic attitude toward life (inability to cope, a lack of initiative and achievement motivation, feelings of alienation, helplessness, dependence, and inferiority). When statistically tested, no relationship between the structure of the families from which these women came and their levels of self-esteem was found.

Bertram P. Karon, in *The Negro Personality* in 1958, said that mother-headed families were partly a carry-over from slavery (where the mother–child bond was allowed to develop, whereas the father–child bond was discouraged).

He states that in Southern cities, the mother-headed family that prevails has more of the character of disorganized family structure; and in Northern cities, the mother-headed family and "loose sexuality, although frequent, is simply a pathological and disorganized form of the general American family structure."

It is not easy to know what goes on inside a family without being a member, yet my data show that black women also get emotional support from their fathers. But why have social scientists placed so much emphasis on absent black fathers rather than on those who are present? Some black fathers still are present in the home (Erikson 1966). For the women in my sample, these black fathers provided emotional and moral support. My respondents generally reported that their fathers often encouraged them to get an education, get ahead, and make something of themselves. This, again, suggests a means for coping. In other words, the women in my sample are getting emotional support from people whom society says are not even around!

For some of my subjects, both emotional and material support from their fathers/father substitutes was invaluable. Some of the responses follow:

> *"He gave me all the things I needed."*
>
> *"He bought everything I needed for school."*
>
> *"He always looked out for the family in every way."*
>
> *"He taught me the right way to go in life."*
>
> *"He provided needed 'push' for continuing my education."*

A Michigan woman, age 24, with one child, said: "My father showed interest in me and taught me to believe that anything worth having is obtainable if one works for it."

One woman reported that her father was unable to give her the extra financial help that she needed; however, she stated that "he stressed the importance of having a good education, keeping good moral behavior, and self-pride."

A Mississippi woman said, "Father gave me a sense of confidence in myself."

Still another lady indicated that "he talked to me a lot and always said to 'be a lady.' "

Other responses about the emotional and material support received from fathers/father substitutes included:

"Even though he was only my stepfather, he provided for me as if I were his real child. I never wanted for anything."

"Father gave me a start in life—a little money and some furniture."

Father always said, "Be honest with yourself and others."

"Father made a down payment on a home for me after my husband and I broke up."

One black woman reported that she felt particularly good about the way in which her father and grandmother (her mother substitute) got along after her mother died.

Although my subjects generally reported that the most admired man in their lives was the father/father substitute, they also looked to other immediate family members for emotional support. Strong family ties have always been a source of support and strength (Hill 1971) in black America.

Not only family ties have been a source of strength for black women but also the church and the clergy. Since slavery, the church has been a viable institution in the lives of black people. The views of the black women in my sample support this contention. The majority of the women felt that the church and religion helped to prepare them for getting ahead in life. Responses as to how the church and religion helped them included:

"The Lord would always show me the way to go."

"Got to have something to believe in, in order to get ahead, and I believe in spiritual things."

"When you pray to the Lord, he will help you."

"Whatever anyone gets out of life comes from God."

A 65-year-old Mississippi divorcee from a second marriage and the mother of two children said: "I paid attention to sermons and songs to pick out something to keep me going. I feel that it gave me hope when I could depend on nobody." Other responses included:

A 24-year-old Michigan mother of one with three years of college said, "Because it taught me that each person has worth, and therefore I feel that we each must strive not only to show our worth—at the same time demand respect for our worth."

A 46-year-old ADC mother of three said, "When I go to church, I just feel better."

Another 23-year-old divorcee said, "You need the sense (or feeling) of God with you to get through everyday life."

The words of a 52-year-old divorcee were: "I do believe in Christianity, for with God by your side, all things are possible. . . . So without religion, you won't get far in life."

Another woman said that religion taught her to be "honest with myself, God, and my fellow man—and I will have success."

"It helps me to believe in God."

"Because God has no respect of person. If anybody else can make it in life, I can too."

"Things in life I have learned to accept and understand, believing that whatever happens is God's will."

These examples support the notion that aside from other black women, mothers/mother substitutes, fathers/father substitutes, and other family members, the church gives black women something to believe in while enabling them to cope with unpleasant situations. Other sources of support for the black women in my study were relatives other than the mother, father, sister, or brother—namely, aunts, uncles, grandmothers, and grandfathers.

Children also act as social support systems. A friend of

mine, a single woman who recently had a baby girl, told me that when she mentioned her pregnancy to an uncle, he said: "It's about time—because you need a baby." His response to her pregnancy suggests that having a child gives women someone to be responsible for. It also implies that people place value on having a child whether the mother is married to the father of the child or not. Even though I did not ask the women in my study a question about the importance of having children, the fact that most of them ranked the role of "being a mother" as of primary importance indicated that having a child is a source of social support.

5

FEELING GOOD
ABOUT ROLES

When we know what a person needs to do in order to think well of herself, we know a lot about that person (Faunce 1972). Throughout life, all of us play numerous roles. How we feel about ourselves is due largely to the levels of success we achieve while performing these roles.

Some women may get a tremendous amount of self-esteem from being a top model, a corporate lawyer, a college professor, a cashier, or a housewife. But it is not likely that all women get the same feeling of self-worthiness from being or even doing various things at a given time in life. A 61-year-old unemployed divorcee who had a ninth-grade education said, "I might not be educated and able to express things, but I am as good as anybody else." What does this comment suggest? To me, this woman was saying that to some people, being educated means being able to express themselves, resulting in a good self-image. I said to myself, "Some supposedly educated people are not capable of expressing themselves and don't have a good image of themselves either." Being educated was not available to her or used by her as an aid in feeling as good as anybody else; the one mechanism that was available to her was "being a mother," which she ranked of first importance. Being the mother of six children, two of whom still lived with her, she told me that she felt very successful as a mother. She said, "I know that I gave my children the best teaching that anyone could have given their children, and I can say this truthfully."

Sometimes when we have a lot of things to "be" and "do" and try to be successful at "being" and "doing" all of them, one or several of those things will surely go lacking in some manner, leaving us not feeling very good about ourselves. In other words, we are not as successful in some roles as we are in others, and there is no need for us to try to fool ourselves into believing that we are. On the other hand, it should not be assumed that we evaluate ourselves on the basis of our success in *any one particular role that society has said should be of extreme importance*, but that we tend to see success in roles that matter to us.

What we think of ourselves is a product of our social experiences, which are organized around all of our social roles in everyday life—for example, being mothers, wives, providers, friends, and so forth. However, the black women I talked to indicated that for them, all roles are not equally important for developing and maintaining a positive self-image. They suggested that they select certain roles from a number of possibilities based on how well they fulfill those roles. The black women, and specifically the heads of families, felt that their level of self-esteem was affected by the value they placed on performing particular roles that "count." This notion is called "role selectivity." One scholar whose works support the notion of "role selectivity" states:

> Although widely overlooked in self-esteem studies, it is a fairly obvious point that a man's global self-esteem is not based solely on his assessment of his constituent qualities; it is based on his self-assessment of qualities that count. (Rosenberg, 1968:339)

Many black women are combining occupations with heading families and are meeting with success at both ends. Being the head of a family seems to bring on a sense of self-worthiness. The heads of families are performing a role that they perceive to be important or worthwhile! They come to feel good about *themselves* as a result of having successfully completed a desired goal. It is rewarding to a mother to send her children to school in nice clothes. There is an added benefit—it makes the children happy, thereby providing another source of satisfaction, since her biggest concern is the happiness of her children. The working, unmarried mother who successfully combined the two roles saw her role as being a "good provider" for her family.

Black-women heads of families, both employed and unemployed, observed that being a "good provider" as well as a disciplinarian or counselor to their children was the most important goal to them.

An unmarried black woman who was a cashier in a department store in Mississippi told me that she had accepted the fact that she has to work because "an honest living is a virtue." She said that everyday when she went to work, she knew that she was going for a reason that came before going to help herself: that was "to take care of Sherrie and Joe," her children. She went on to say that she felt good in knowing that they didn't have to ask anyone for anything because "they know that they have a mother to take care of them."

Pat, who lived in Michigan, a mother of four children, had been separated from her husband for three years. She did not work. However, she did receive support from the children's father. Pat said that her children's livelihood was most important to her, because she knew they were her responsibility when it came to discipline. She stated that she decided immediately following the separation from her husband that their children's pattern of living would come more from the things that *she* taught them than from anything else. She continuously emphasized instilling love in her children and the knowledge of managing a home as best one can with limited funds.

Of all the women I talked to, the working women were more likely to define successful motherhood on the basis of being a "good provider" than those who did not work. Interestingly enough, the unemployed mothers were more likely to cite raising their children in defining success as a mother. But both groups of women seemed to have an alternative for developing a feeling of worth in coping.

Whereas the employed heads of families saw family maintenance and provider roles as available to them in coping, the unemployed heads of families only had the family maintenance role. The unemployed women felt that even though they did not have jobs, they were still providing for and maintaining their families on what they did have; thus, they also chose the mother role as being of first importance. For example:

> *Olivia, a 28-year-old divorcee, saw success as a mother in that, "I make sure my children are adequately provided for with the income that I have."*
>
> *Another woman said, "I am a successful mother in that I am always able to cooperate with my children as well as chastise them."*
>
> *One woman, age 65, said: "I'm successful as a mother in training my children in the right way and teaching them to work for what they get. Really, I don't know of any unsuccessful things."*
>
> *A Michigan woman said: "I must be successful in that I have raised three grown children and six grandchildren, all on welfare and by myself. I raised them on welfare, and that in itself gives you an idea of what I had to endure."*
>
> *One unemployed head of a family stated: "I give my children my attention, no matter what I am doing around the house. When I listen to them and train them in the way that they should go, they will do alright in later life."*
>
> *A 37-year-old divorcee with three children from Michigan who was a secretary replied; "I have to work in order to take care of my children, and I do just that.*

I love my children first—and I could not show them as much love as I want to show them if I could not give them the things which they need."

Another working head of a family saw success as a mother by "providing a good home life for my children—materially, spiritually, morally, and emotionally."

A 58-year-old widow. who bought a building while working as a beautician in Michigan, which she later converted into a restaurant that she operated, said, "I am successful as a mother because my two children (sons) are off in graduate school and I had to bring them up by myself since their father died eleven years ago."

Other comments included:

"I try to give my child what he needs to grow physically and mentally."

"I do my best as a mother to my four children—and I think my best is very good in the line of what little money that I get plus the love that I give them."

"Any woman who has kids should try to do all she can for them by showing them love and understanding—whether she works or not."

"I feel I am successful as a mother because I do things with my children when I am not at work. Too, we (she and her children) are honest with each other. We can talk and reason with each other—and that makes me feel good as their mother."

Still other general comments included "showing love to (their) children," "teaching them responsibility and to make something of themselves," and "how to get along with people."

Looking at the responses from unemployed heads of families, it is important to note that not all were on welfare; there were other sources of income that included disability payments, Social Security, income from relatives, child support, renters (for property owners), and retirement. As long as these women had food, clothing, and shelter for their children, they were *providing* for them—through whatever means. There are alternatives available to each group of women who head up their families. For the employed, there is first the mother role, which is enhanced by the provider role. For the unemployed, there is also the mother role, which is enhanced by whatever source of finance is available to them.

ROLE CONFLICT

Try answering the telephone, disciplining your two children—ages 3 and 5—who have been with a babysitter most of the day, while burning the dinner—which should be at least three-fourths ready when your husband returns from work at 6:30 P.M. You probably feel that these are unrealistic experiences. Yet they somewhat parallel working, mothering, wifing, and whatever else you have to do. For some women, and especially for black women with husbands who are assumed to be the heads of their families by the general public, the experiences are very real.

People experience role conflict when the roles placed upon them are incompatible, thus making it uncomfortable, even impossible, for them to fulfill all sets of expectations at the same time. And for black women who are married, working and being a mother, a wife, a friend, and so on must make for unpleasant experiences. I had actually assumed that when anybody attempts to meet at least two sets of expectations that contradict each other, personal and interpersonal disruption would be a common outcome. This is not to "knock" the notion of being married; I personally feel that it is a great institution.

To work or not to work? That has been an agonizing question for many women who are not the heads of their families. The reason for the agony is that fulfilling both roles may produce some conflict between the two. (It used to be widely believed that women's only role was inside the home.) Therefore, if she found satisfaction outside the home and a small crisis occurred inside it, she could be made to feel quite guilty. I had assumed that these women may, and often do, experience role conflict because they attempt to succeed in both occupational and mother roles. Conflict between roles that involve the woman deeply is certain to reduce the likelihood of success in performing any of the roles, thus making it difficult for her to maintain self-esteem. Employed women who are the heads of their families are less likely to experience role conflicts, because the *necessity* of working to provide for their families is tied to being a good mother.

The two roles that working mothers who are the heads of their families combined were being a mother and being employed, and being employed and able to provide for their children added to their feelings about being a "good mother." Even though these women, as most of the others in the sample, ranked being a mother as being of first importance, they saw being employed as adding to their fulfillment as mothers.

One woman stated that her first obligation was to her child and her second, to working in order to take care of her child. She feels successful as a mother because she's independent and is able to give him some of the things he wants and needs.

A 37-year-old divorcee who worked as a medical technician said that being a mother is first and foremost in her life. Secondly, she's proud to be qualified to hold a job in order to take care of her children. She also indicated that she does a better job of taking care of her children than some black women with husbands.

A 52-year-old nurses' aide who made only $270 a month (take home) said she was successful in providing for her children because she managed the financial situation "pretty well."

My data clearly show that working nonheads of families are more likely to be dissatisfied about spending time away from their children than employed heads of families. I have also determined that black married women, in most instances, find it *necessary* to work outside the home in order to supplement their husbands' incomes to provide for their families. Employed heads of families are more likely than employed non-heads of families to be satisfield about spending time away from their children. These data strongly suggest that married working mothers are more likely to experience role conflict than unmarried working mothers.

Now we want to get some idea of how women who are not the heads of families, or whose husbands are present in the home, tend to define success as a mother. I made an assumption, then set out to prove or disprove it. The assumption was that women who are not the heads of families and who are unemployed use values that relate to being a mother as the primary basis for deciding how they feel about themselves.

Overall, my findings suggest that women who are the heads of families place more value on their role as provider, whereas those who are not the the heads of families place greater value on their role as mother. Donna, the nonworking wife of a prominent medical doctor, said:

"It gives me great pleasure to stay at home and watch my own kids grow up. Being there when their small problems arise is satisfying to me because I am on the spot whenever a question arises that must be dealt with immediately." Donna, who was not responsible for providing the material needs of her children, was able to devote all her time and efforts to "mothering" them.

Every woman in my study group had a role that she felt was more important to her than others. And whether those roles were as mothers, wives, or workers, each woman felt that fulfilling that role was worthwhile to others as well as to herself. In her own way, each woman had found her ideal mechanism for coping with life in a complex society. With each measure of success, each of the subjects was able to experience feeling good about her role and about herself.

Because being a mother and being a wife are not one and the same, in reality, when the women were asked to rank the two roles, their regarding both as of first importance suggested role conflict. Consequently, these were also the women who ranked working or being employed as being of second importance. A 53-year-old woman said, "Being a wife and mother go together." She saw her success as a mother as having successfully reared her children and her success as a wife, as not having been divorced. Having ranked being employed as being of second importance, she said: "Working keeps me from being idle, and friends (ranked of third importance) may get you in trouble."

Other responses on the importance of being a wife included:

> *One woman who ranked the importance of being a wife first stated: "Being a wife and mother can be very gratifying or defective, depending on the individual. I try to make my part as wife-mother a good one; therefore I acquire self-satisfaction in knowing I am doing my best."*

> *Another woman noted that "being a wife is my most important job right now. I know that motherhood should be important in every woman's life. Having friends is important to me mentally, but I rated employment last."*

> *Another woman said that "being a mother is most important. Anybody can be a wife." She said that her children come first in terms of the things that they can provide for them—the essentials as well as the luxuries. However, she defines success as a wife in these terms: "I put my husband's needs, wants, and aspirations before my own."*

One woman said: "One should be a good wife first and then a good mother to her children. Having a job is very important, too, because you need money to live. You can have lots of friends and work too." This woman also stated that her success as a mother was that she felt more like a sister to the baby than a mother. This particular case might suggest a way of repressing role conflict. She feels successful as a wife because she "keeps the home in good shape, works to provide things for the home, and prepares good meals."

A 29-year-old employed mother said, "Being a mother comes first because my children need me more than my husband does." She defined success as a wife as being "very understanding and a good homemaker."

One 35-year-old woman said that "you have to be a good wife in order to be a good mother."

A 23-year-old mother of two said that "being a mother is more important than being a wife in that the children cannot take care of themselves. Having a job is of next importance in order to supplement the family income."

One woman who ranked being a mother first and a wife second stated: "Even though I was a wife before I was a mother, my children need me more now."

Another woman, age 49, who worked as a nurses' aide in Mississippi and who ranked being a wife and mother as equally important said: "Being a wife is the most important thing in my life. As a working mother, I reared my children quite well, but I wish I didn't

> *have to work—then I could be a better mother. I could also be a better wife if I didn't work."*
>
> *One woman who ranked being a wife first and a mother second said she loves her children and that by being employed, she can help provide for the home. However, she saw herself as an unsuccessful wife in that she was "being too independent and unsuccessful in maintaining the home."*
>
> *One 47-year-old woman said she wanted to be a wife first and then a mother. She viewed success as a wife in that she had a husband and somewhere to live."*
>
> *A 40-year-old mother of two who was a salesperson at a leading chain store ranked being a wife of first importance, saying: "My first duty is to my husband and then to my children. I am a good mother, but I don't see my children enough because I have to work late sometimes."*
>
> *A woman whose husband was a shoe repairman said, "I can't be a wife without being a mother; neither can I be a mother without being a wife."*

The preceding cases, in addition to several others, might lead one to believe that dissatisfaction about time spent away from children due to working indicates role conflict and a feeling of being less successful as a mother. So I asked both women who were the heads of families and those who were married, employed nonheads of families how they felt about the time spent away from their children, even though it was spent working to provide for them. The majority of the heads of families indicated that they were very satisfied; however, the married employed women stated that they were less than satisfied.

Since it is my belief that our evaluation of ourselves as the heads of our families is based on combining the good provider and family maintenance roles, we are less likely to experience role conflict. Why? Knowing that we are the ones who, in most instances, must provide while being mothers to our children, we view success in those terms— roles that we have to fulfill. Because we do not have to be wives, there can exist no conflict between these roles. Moreover, as stated earlier, the provider role, for the heads of families, serves as a reinforcement of the mother role; that is, "By working, I am able to provide for my children."

Like the unemployed family heads, married women who do not work use the family maintenance role as a primary basis for coping. They too were asked to rank the roles of being a wife, mother, employed, or having lots of friends. The majority of them ranked being a mother as most important.

A 30-year-old Michigan mother of five children said: "My kids come before anybody. Being a wife means a lot to me, too, but working is not very important in that I budget the money that my husband makes and put it to good use."

Another woman said she views success as a mother as of most importance in that she teaches her children "right from wrong, keeps them off the streets and out of trouble."

A Michigan woman who stayed home to take care of

her two children ranked being a wife as of first importance and being a mother, second. She also said that if she had to work to help her husband support her family, being employed would be of more importance than having lots of friends. In defining her success as a wife, she said: "I can keep the home comfortable and try to make ends meet for all of us. Some weeks, we don't have as much as we do other weeks, but I manage the money and we make it."

After having ranked being a mother as most important, a 27-year-old mother of two said, "My children probably need me more than anyone else." She defines herself as a successful mother "in all ways" and as a successful wife by "providing a happy home."

The wife of a medical doctor and mother of four children considered being a wife and being a mother as equally important. She indicated that since she did not have to work, she could be more of a wife to her husband and a mother to her children while the husband provided.

One woman even said that "being a wife is being decent."

Another said: "Being a wife is of first importance to me, even though I have not kept my streamlined figure, but I hope my husband doesn't wander."

A woman whose husband was a construction worker felt that she was successful as a wife and mother because she took care of the financial matters for her husband.

These women, even though unemployed and not having to serve as the heads of their families, had the family maintenance role available to them.

In reality, most black women can ill afford to stay home because of the necessity of supplementing the family income. Unlike the employed married women and heads of families, this group of women may or may not have freedom of choice in terms of associates, or at least may or may not have freedom in *exercising* that choice. Does she turn to soap operas in getting an image of herself, or is she like other black women who identify with persons in similar situations? No, black women heads of families do *not* have to compare themselves with white women in male-headed families. True, it might be easier for some women than for others to avoid this comparison. For example, if your nextdoor neighbor, someone you work with, or anyone else you cannot avoid seeing is a white woman in a male-headed family, then this comparison is more likely to be made. Similarly, if you cannot avoid seeing people who share the views of Moynihan and others, then it may difficult to avoid the stigmatizing effects of these views. However, I believe it is not the general kind of society we live in, but the specific people we see most often and by whom we are most frequently evaluated who have the most effect on our self-images. We do have some freedom in picking our associates, and to the extent that we use that freedom, we are likely to pick friends who will measure us on the things we would like to be evaluated on and refrain from assessing us on things we do not consider important. We cannot always choose the people we see most often. This is especially true for employed black women. But it is also true for unemployed heads of families who must deal with the welfare system.

I asked the 400 black women of this sample: "When thinking of yourself as a successful or unsuccessful mother, wife, or provider, with what group of women do you compare yourself?" At least 96 percent of the women said that they compared themselves with other black women in general, or with other black women they knew. Responses to why they made this selection included:

> *"I know them better."*
>
> *"I'm proud to be black."*
>
> *"Because I've been around blacks all my life."*
>
> *"Because they're black, too."*
>
> *"They most likely do some of the same things that I do."*
>
> *"Because we've had to struggle for a long time."*
>
> *"I think that all black women are alike in most ways.*
>
> *"I associate generally more with blacks."*
>
> *"Because I can communicate better with black women."*
>
> *"Because I want to be compared with blacks."*
>
> *"Because I'm black, and I know black women who have worked just as hard as I have."*
>
> *"Because I feel that we have the same problems."*
>
> *"I can relate to my own people."*
>
> *"Because they're more helpful to me."*

As stated previously, people in similar situations who share similar experiences get images of themselves from one another. I asked the women of my sample to rank the group of women with whom they would like to be compared. From the choices of black women who were heads of families, black women who had husbands, white women who were heads of families, and white women who had husbands, 77 percent of the heads of families and 10 percent of the married women said that they would like to be compared with black-women heads of families; whereas 23 percent of the heads of families and 90 percent of the married women chose to be compared with black women who had husbands. Responses from black-women heads of families follow:

A 30-year-old divorcee who identified with black-women heads of families said, "Because I have accomplished just as much as they have."

A 43-year-old divorcee chose other women who were heads of families because she "feels that we have something in common."

A 24-year-old woman who was separated from her husband chose other black-women heads of families. When asked why, she said, "Because I feel that I am a person of worth just as these women are."

One 27-year-old divorcee from Mississippi said "because being heads of families implies that we serve as models for the building of respect and responsibility for our children. I want to be compared to that group of women."

A Michigan divorcee, age 44, said, "I feel that I'm worth an awful lot, because I'm doing a good job of raising my children, too."

One woman who asked to be compared to black-women heads of families said, "Some of us are doing a better job with our families than women with husbands."

Another woman, comparing herself with black-women heads of families, said, "I am a person of worth because I've always had a meaning in life—which we all should have."

A 58-year-old widow gave the following as the reason for her choice of women: "Because I am also a black woman who heads my family."

Another black family head who chose to be compared to other black-women heads of families said, "Because I think I'm just as good as those women and better than some."

Married women responding about feeling worthy as compared to other married women also gave reasons for their choices:

A 47-year-old Michigan woman said, "Because I feel that I'm doing just as good and am as good as anyone else."

One woman, age 24, said she's "on the same level with them."

A 27-year-old said, "Because I'm worth just as much as anyone else."

Another woman, age 42, said, "Because I'm fortunate enough to play the mother role and the wife role successfully."

One 45-year-old Michigander responded, "Because I am a black woman, and I am worth as much as the women in the group that I picked."

A Michigan woman who was 41 years old said, "Because I like myself."

Another, age 47, said, "They all tell me I do a good job."

A 52-year-old woman said, "Because I feel secure, not inferior."

A 49-year-old Mississippi native presently living in Michigan said, "I'm just as good and important as anyone."

Other responses included:

"We both have to be a lot of things to our families."

"We are alike in that we have to push our husbands."

"Black married women are one of a kind."

Our experiences as black women go beyond our lack of recognition by the larger society; we do, in fact, identify with one another. Not only does the existing literature suggest that as black-women heads of families, having one another to identify with, we cannot cope with being black and female at the same time; that literature also tells us that we place more value on our daughters than on our sons. Such a stereotypical notion could add to our inability to cope if being *unable* to cope were the case for us.

THE MYTH
OF BLACK
EMASCULATION

Within white America, there exists the belief that most black families are dominated by black women and that these women do a job of "putting down" black men. However, the assumption that black men have been castrated or put down by black women has yet to be proved.

True, the myth of black emasculation lingers. As suggested by Staples:

> One can see in this myth an unmitigated fear of Black male power, and unrelenting determination on the part of white America to create in fiction what it has been unable to accomplish in the empirical world. (1971:2–3)

The mere fact that this myth lingers could also deter our ability to cope as black-women heads of families. However, it has not done so. Setting one's sights on what is most important and ignoring all outside influences that conflict with those goals is the key to the doctrine of role expectations for sons of black women. How can we have certain role expectations for our sons and emasculate them at the same time?

This chapter is an attempt to counteract the effects of the myth of black emasculation by offering a descriptive account of black mothers' role expectations for their sons. In other words, the women I talked to wanted "good things" to happen to their sons as well as to their daughters.

Role expectations are the ways that people believe they must behave in particular situations. The expectations are determined by the anticipated outcome, and they are shared by the mothers of sons.

How do we account for the achievements of the black men of today and not realize that they are *sons of black women?* These are the same black women whom society has labeled as castraters.

Upon what experiences do black women's role expectations for their sons depend? I asked the women of my samples if there was any particular kind of job they would like their sons to have more than any other. Results showed that for the Michigan sample, a greater proportion of unmarried women (68 percent) than married women had particular jobs in mind for their sons. However, for the Mississippi sample, both married and unmarried women stated that they had particular jobs in mind for their sons, 83 percent and 74 percent, respectively. It is also important that among those women who said yes to having a particular job in mind, examples of the kinds of jobs specified were executive, doctor (M.D. or Ph.D), musician, lawyer, teacher, social worker, artist, electrician, and professional athlete. Among the respondents who said they did not have a particular kind of job in mind, the no responses were accompanied by the statement: "Any job which provides security and with which he is happy."

Living in a world where their chances for getting ahead were not good, the majority of the black women said that their sons' chances for "getting ahead" were much better or somewhat better than their chances have been. However, for the Mississippi sample, a greater proportion (90 percent) of the heads of families than of married women (79 percent) said that their son's chances were better or somewhat better than their own. These so-labeled "black-male castraters" were certainly optimistic about their sons' chances for good things happening to them.

A college education apparently was felt to be of great importance in preparing for a career, since the majority of black women stated that their sons' chances for going to college were excellent or good. The greatest proportion of the women who felt that their sons' chances were excellent or good also stated that they encouraged their sons to go to college.

Counseling their sons and training them religiously served as a "way of life" for the women of the samples. Many of the women felt that they exposed their sons to *more* religious training than other families they knew. However, the majority (60 percent) said that their sons were exposed to the *same* religious training as most families they knew. In addition to religious exposure, the mothers stated that the most important thing their sons should do to prepare themselves for life was to "think for themselves."

Whereas most of the women—both heads of families and married women—had high expectations of their sons, this does not mean that black men do not also have some direct, positive effect on the rearing of sons. It simply means that black women are capable of providing the necessary tools, both tangible and intangible, for their sons to survive within a *society* that emasculates them. It also means that when a man is not continuously available to sons within the family, the strengths of black women may serve as positive forces for their sons' survival. Additionally, this does not necessarily mean that black-women heads of families aspire to serve as positive survival forces by themselves; continued negative forces of society compel them to do so. In reality, it is generally society that attempts to emasculate black men—not us.

*Parts of this chapter appear as "On Marital Relations: Perceptions of Black Women" by Lena Wright Myers in *Black Women* (SAGE FOCUS EDITION Volume 21), La Frances Rodgers- Rose, Editor, pp. 161-72. Copyright 1980. They are reprinted by permission of the Publisher, Sage Publications, Inc. (Beverly Hills/London).

BLACK WOMEN
BLACK MEN
RELATIONSHIPS*

During the past few years, a number of books have been written about different aspects of human sexuality. "How-to-do-it" manuals have become best-sellers, and books on sex roles and the psychology or social psychology of women (usually whites) have become household items. Recently, a few authors have started discussing the many supposedly profound and difficult dilemmas of intimate relationships and love that are evolving between men and women. And the latter term, *love*, has been claimed to be so subjective and so elusive that it defies definition. As a matter of fact, there are almost as many ways to love as there are people in the world to love and be loved by. True, expressions of love vary from culture to culture, era to era, and person to person. In some centuries, "real love" had to be romantic and free of the "ugliness" of sex. In other periods, intimate expression was considered the most important ingredient of love.

Attitudes toward intimate expressions in the Western world have varied between the extremes of an almost total suppression of sexuality—at least on the surface—and a public tolerance of all varieties of intimate expression. The mass media have given emotional expression with overtones of sexuality the hard sell, processing and packaging it in a variety of styles.

One may review magazine articles to see how the stars express themselves intimately. Another person may examine orthodox cases of intimacy by various religious groups. Others may seek the norms of close friends or peers or may revert to parental norms regarding intimate expression. But we all must set our own course for expressing ourselves in an intimate relationship.

Maybe some people are "on the fringes" in the search for their own personal, emotional expressions of sexuality (Masters and Johnson 1974:86).

This chapter is not an effort to define love among black men and black women; nor is it an attempt to provide a "how-to-do-it" (whatever it is that you are doing at a given time) manual. It is simply a descriptive account of social interaction among black couples as told by 400 black women. Now what is meant by social interaction?

Developing and weaving concepts, Mead (1934) noted that social interaction may be viewed as a conversation of gestures. He suggested that a conversation of gestures includes the mutual adjustment of behavior, where each partner uses the *first* action of the other partner to determine her or his next move. Thus, her or his response becomes a stimulus to the other partner, prompting either a change in the other partner's attitude or the completion of the originally intended act. One person may unconsciously respond to the tone of voice or facial expression of the person with whom he or she is interacting, and the other person may be unaware of that response at a given time. This is called unconscious or nonsignificant conversation of gestures, and it consists of simple stimulus and response. But through the process of socialization, most human interaction becomes symbolic, depending upon shared understandings about the meanings of actions. People respond to their environment by interpreting the actions of others. They do not respond mechanically to the intrinsic qualities of situations. Instead, they assign meanings to the situation at hand and respond in terms of those meanings (Blumer 1966). We learn to assign meaning to given situations while interacting with other persons. "Since each person will respond to events in terms of the meanings he or she assigns to them, each person's action is comprehensible and predictable to others only to the degree that the underlying meanings are *known*" (Lauer and Handel 1977).

Social interaction is defined in this chapter as a social process that stresses communication through language and gestures (body talk) in the formation and maintenance of personality and social relationship among black men and black women. I am saying that there are many things that are left *unsaid* among black women and men. This may even complement the old cliché that "action speaks louder than words." True, some things need to go *unsaid* and *unacted*, too, if there is not shared symbolic meaning among women and men in the form of language and gestures. However, if there are shared symbolic meanings, both verbally and nonverbally, more positive relationships may exist between black women and black men.

Most blacks do not marry in pursuit of a secure financial status, as whites often do, but when they do, they could end up as described by Ladner (1971):

> It could be that when Blacks fall into the "trap" of using the dominant society's reasons for marriage, they become "ipso facto" prone to failure, because in this kind of environment, emotional love cannot counteract joblessness and the multitude of tensions which are frequently present.

For many blacks, the realities of the world cause frustrations that have some impact on their love life. Therefore, it may be necessary to find alternatives for coping with the negative influences of society. Let us assume that a kind of intimacy exists that creates an unconscious desire for black married couples to retain their marital relationships rather than dissolve them. This form of symbolic intimacy may exist in spite of negative environmental influences and traditional norms. This chapter describes how these black women in my study saw their social relationships with their husbands or former husbands.

One of the expressive gratifications sought by married couples is cathectic affection. In order to examine how satisfied black women were with their cathectic affection, the following question was asked:

Cathectic affection has to do with feelings or emotions pertaining to the physical aspect of married life. These may range from the most innocent to the most intimate demonstrations of affection. Now then, are you generally satisfied or dissatisfied with this aspect of your marriage or former marriage?

For both samples, the married women appear more satisfied with the cathectic aspect of their marriages than do the women who are separated or divorced. The difference between the married women and the single women (separated or divorced) of the Mississippi sample is only slight (94 percent and 91 percent, respectively). But for the Michigan sample, the difference between the married women and single women is much greater. Ninety-six percent of the married women expressed general satisfaction with their cathectic affection, whereas 68 percent of the single women expressed the same satisfaction.

A clearer understanding of cathectic affection may be found in the examples that follow.

Faye was a 47-year-old married woman with four children who lived in Mississippi. Faye had no problems discussing her marital relationship with Melvin (her husband) with me. She said, "Melvin has a way of looking at me that tells me that he wants to be with *me*, without having to say one word." She also said that he had another way of looking at her that let her know he did not want to be bothered at times.

Somewhat related is the example of Gerri, a native of Michigan, age 30, a divorcee and the mother of one child. She talked about how "touchy-feely" both she and Paul (her former husband) had been. Gerri made it very clear that the lack of cathectic affection was not the reason that their marriage ended in divorce. As a matter of fact, she stated, "That is one of the things that I miss the most about Paul and my relationship. . . . We could understand and feel each other."

Both cases indicate shared meanings and understandings of emotional expressions between black women and their husbands or former husbands. Even though Faye may not have been very pleased about the way Melvin looked at her when he did not want to be bothered, she must have understood the nonverbal gesture and likely behaved accordingly. An understanding of such a gesture could also have aided her in not becoming a "clinging vine" in the marital relationship—as some women do and that some men resent.

For Gerri, the nonverbal communication between her and Paul appeared to have been of great importance to their relationship. Being physically affectionate toward each other seems to suggest shared meanings and understanding through and about touching.

The fact that black women were satisfied with the physical affection shown by their mates is symbolic in that there must have been shared understanding about the meaning of gestures. Satisfaction received from expressions of physical affection has meaning and arouses meaning in the partners to whom these expressions are communicated. This sharing is essential to communication in interacting socially with others. As one writer puts it:

> Each part of the body speaks a silent but intimate and revealing language. More than mere words—a wink, a shrug,

or a handclasp can be the best clue you'll ever get to a person's innermost feelings. (Callum 1972:1)

The key to nonverbal communication of emotional expression is understanding the *clues*, and one doesn't have to be a sociologist or a psychologist to do so. Black people are an expressive people. Responses to the previous question indicate that shared meanings and understandings about such clues did exist between black women and their husbands or former husbands, as perceived by the women.

As black married couples speak, they are aware of the response they hope to arouse. Each gesture or word serves as a stimulus to them as well as to their spouses. Now let us examine the women's perception of freedom to communicate with their husbands or former husbands.

Assuming that the "significant other" within a marital situation at a given time is the spouse, the women of these samples were asked the following question:

Do you feel very free _____, free _____, not so free _____ to confide, talk things over, or discuss anything with your husband or former husband?

We find from the responses that the married women of both the Michigan and Mississippi samples felt freer than the separated or divorced women to communicate with their spouses. Conversely, the separated or divorced women felt less free to communicate with their spouses than did the married women. It is interesting to note that the married women of Mississippi felt less free than the married women of Michigan to communicate with their husbands. Could this difference be accounted for by region or social class? This question cannot be answered by this analysis, but it would be an interesting issue to pursue in the future.

Examples of freedom or lack of freedom to communicate verbally with husbands or former husbands follow.

Ellen was a 68-year-old mother of four children from Mississippi, who had been married to George for forty-seven years. She said, "I never believed in the old saying that a woman should be seen but not heard—like some people say about children—and George knows that."

However, Annette, a 28-year-old mother of two from Michigan, made an interesting comment. She had been separated from Ray for almost three years. Annette stated, "He never wanted me to say much of anything unless he asked me something." The lack of verbal communication between Annette and Ray is obvious in that Ray seemed to want Annette to do little or no talking to him. One-way verbal communication (as in this case) must have been extremely frustrating—especially for the listener. This alone could account for Annette having felt "not so free" to confide, talk things over, or discuss anything with her former husband.

Now . . . what is this saying to us? It could be that a distinction between verbal and nonverbal communication did not occur between the separated or divorced women and their former spouses. Or it may be that if distinctions were made, neither form of communication was utilized to its fullest, which may have accounted for the marital relationships being broken.

In an effort to assess the husbands' readiness to understand what their wives say to them during the process of interacting, I asked the women this question:

> Do you feel that your husband/former husband very readily
> _____, readily _____, not so readily _____ receives or under-
> stands what you are trying to say?

A greater proportion of the married women than of the separated or divorced women in both samples said that their husbands very readily received or understood what they were trying to say to them. Conversely, a greater proportion of the separated or divorced women than of the married women indicated that their former husbands did *not* so readily receive or understand what they were trying to say.

The difference between the married women and the separated or divorced women is much greater in the Michigan sample than in the Mississippi sample. In other words, the Mississippi women, the married as well as the separated or divorced, are more similar to one another 49 percent, 40 percent) than are the Michigan women (85 percent, 42 percent) with regard to their perceptions of husbands' empathy.

Companionship is a form of expressive gratification that is sought in marriage. In order to test this, the following question was asked:

> Companionship has to do with shared leisure or non-work-
> time activities—e.g. movies, picnics, parties, and dancing.
> Are you generally satisfied _____ or dissatisfied _____ with this
> aspect of your marriage or former marriage?

The responses show that a greater proportion of married women were satisfied with their companionship than women who were separated or divorced for both the Michigan and Mississippi black women. The difference between married and single women is greater in the Michigan sample (90 percent and 56 percent, respectively) than in the Mississippi sample (67 percent and 49 percent, respectively). A 52-year-old divorcee from Michigan said that her former husband was never home long enough to do anything with her and their six children, even when he was not at work. This confirms what is commonly expected. That is, if separated or divorced women were satisfied with their marriages, they would still be married, especially in that companionship is the essence of marriage.

Interacting individuals in any situation must constantly interpret the gestures of others, and in doing so, they adjust their own intentions, wishes, feelings, and attitudes. This process of interpretation and redefinition relates to all kinds of interpersonal situations, whether they involve cooperation, love, conflict, hostility, or anger. This notion was examined by using the following questions:

> How often would you say that you and your husband/former husband had a big "blow-up" and really got angry with each other?
>
> ____never   ____sometimes   ____very often
> ____seldom   ____often

Responses showed that married women in the Michigan sample were more likely than the separated or divorced women to experience little marital conflict. On the other hand, the separated or divorced women were more likely to have had more conflicts with their former husbands. This conforms to a commonsense expectation. Conflict is negatively related to marital disruption, although some conflict is positively related to a marriage.

In the Mississippi sample, we find that neither the married nor the single women (separated or divorced) had no marital conflicts. Nevertheless, the married women experienced conflicts less often than did the single women (26 percent and 52 percent, respectively).

The notion of conflict in a marital relationship brings to mind an article that appeared in a magazine some time ago and included a request for advice from a marriage counselor. It is titled "Problems Remain the Same."

> After ten years of marriage, our problems today are the same as at the beginning. It seems that there can be no compromise. Briefly, our problems are:
>
> 1. He thinks I talk too much detail. He tunes me out, and does not remember things I have told him.
> 2. He says I depend on him too much for little decisions.
> 3. I don't like to argue. I used to cry over misunderstandings, which disgusted him. Now I sulk.
> 4. I have always been more affectionate than he— sometimes too aggressive, which annoys him. I have restrained myself, but this has not made him more affectionate. . . .
>
> *(Home Life Magazine,* 1974:15-17)
> Signed, Lonely

Conflict is often viewed negatively. However, some theorists suggest that conflict has some positive aspects (Simmel 1955). It can serve as a force that integrates people on opposing sides, bonding them firmly into a group. Granted, this applies to at least two people interacting. Thus, conflict may be advantageous to some black married couples in that they may refrain from personal abuse (currently called spouse battering) and confine a quarrel to issues, thus eliminating points of tension. In addition, it may bring husbands and wives into communication with one another, forcing them to face up to their problems.

In examining reasons for conflict among the women and their husbands or former husbands, the following questions were asked:

What is/was this usually about?
    ____occupational and financial matters
    ____others (specify) _____

and

Thinking back over your married life, what was the *one* thing that you and your husband or former husband have disagreed about more than others?*

_____

_____

The responses show the issues over which the women had marital conflicts. For the Michigan married women, "suspicion of husband playing around on wife," followed by occupational or financial matters, were the issues on which they had the greatest conflicts. The issues over which they

---

*It is important to note that responses to this open-ended question were also used in pursuing data on "communication" between the women and their husbands/former husbands, where responses regarding "communicating" occurred.

had the fewest conflicts were discipline of children and infrequent sexual activity on the part of the husband (11 percent each). For the single women, the greatest conflict occurred over occupational or financial issues, followed by "suspicion of husband playing around on wife." This pattern is just the reverse for the married women, as already noted. The issues over which the single women had the least conflict were "infrequent sexual activity on the part of the husband," followed by discipline of the children.

For the Mississippi sample, we find some variations from the Michigan sample. The married women of Mississippi seem to have their greatest marital conflict over discipline of children, followed by "suspicion of husband playing around on wife." The former issue was one of the issues least leading to marital conflict among the Michigan sample. The issue over which the least conflict occurred was "infrequent sexual activity on the part of the husband." For the single women, the conflicts occurred most frequently over "suspicion of husband playing around on wife," followed by occupational or financial matters. The issues over which they had the fewest conflicts were discipline of children and "infrequent sexual activity on the part of the husband."

This chapter is by no means exhaustive. It is an effort to offer a descriptive account of social interaction that exists among black married couples as alternatives that affect the maintenance of their marital relationships, as reported by 400 black women. From the empirical findings, one may conclude that alternatives utilized by black married couples in retaining their marital status include: perceptions of cathectic affection, perceptions of the opportunity to relate to their husbands (thus having them respond favorably), perceived degree of satisfaction with companionship, and the ability of both partners to use conflict to their advantage in the relationship.

In conclusion, black married and unmarried women may see one function of social and symbolic relationships in marriage as a source of emotional support (support system) and concern for someone to confide in. Spouses (mates) seem to fulfill the need that cannot be satisfied by the larger society because of its structure. Let us, too, realize that being divorced or separated does, in many instances, eliminate social and symbolic interaction between black women and black men in a living arrangement. Although sometimes misunderstood by outsiders, memories of this relationship can remain a part of a former black mate's entire life. This was suggested by the 400 women from Michigan and Mississippi.

Black women and black men, as reasoning creatures, can relate to each other verbally and through self-disclosure, can learn something about each other and about their own identities as well. In addition, as sexual creatures, we have the ability to express ourselves—our feelings, thoughts, and even our fantasies—through physical gestures, or rather nonverbal communication. It simply becomes an ongoing process of relating, sharing, and communicating.

SELF-IMAGES
OF BLACK WOMEN

Thus far, I have written a lot about how we, as black-women heads of families, cope with the numerous pressures in everyday life that go along with being black and female. But I have not discussed the general patterns that have reinforced the idea that we do have good images of ourselves as the heads of our families. Some people seem to think that blacks cannot realistically substantiate what we have to say without using highly sophisticated statistics for interpreting human behavior—and especially the behavior of black people.

When I speak of self-esteem and coping, again I mean self-esteem ♦ coping. I am talking about a feeling of self-worth—a feeling that we are *good enough*. Good enough to and for whom? We are good enough to and for ourselves, our families (who count so much in our lives), and our social support systems, whose experiences are similar and whose opinions matter to us more than any others. We simply feel that we are persons of worth and respect ourselves for what we are. We do not need to be told what we should do or with whom we should identify in order to feel *good enough* about ourselves.

Before I began the research for this book, I carefully searched the measures of self-esteem. Unfortunately, I found very little that related to the samples of black women I had planned to interview. The one source that came close to what and how I wanted to measure their levels of self-esteem was Rosenberg's Self-Esteem Scale of 1965. Additionally I used some items from Berger's Self-Acceptance Scale of 1952. These two general models helped me to combine roles and persons black women might have used in developing and maintaining a positive image of themselves.

Some of the self-esteem questions focused on how the women saw themselves when compared with the women with whom they identified, as stated earlier during the interview. For example, when asked if they felt they were persons of worth as compared to those other women, the majority of both samples either "very strongly" or "strongly" agreed that they did. The largest proportion felt that they had a number of good qualities as compared to the other women. Many stated that they were able to do things in general as well as that group of women, again noting other black women. Feeling a sense of pride in themselves, the majority of these women also noted that they had much to be proud of as compared with other women. Less than 20 percent of the black women said that they were inclined to feel that they were failures and only a few stated that they sometimes wished they could have more respect for themselves. These few were black-women heads of families who were unemployed and lived in Michigan. To be satisfied with oneself could imply that one is comfortable with whatever means one uses in coping with adversity. The majority of these black women said that they were satisfied with themselves.

For many individuals, being liked by others lends to building and maintaining self-esteem. A significant number of these women felt that they were liked by most people (the author assumes "most people" means individuals the women knew or who knew them). However, few of the women felt that they had to do what others expected of them in order to be liked by others. Supportive of these women's feelings of worth is the fact that they were not afraid to let peole know what they were really like for fear that other people would be disppointed in them. Consequently, these women did not find it hard to believe the good things that were said about them. If you have confidence in yourself, you can accept compliments without question or doubt.

In response to the inquiry about feeling uncomfortable in social situations, these black women indicated that they did not feel the least bit uncomfortable. Moreover, they experienced no discomfort or shyness when they found themselves in the presence of others whom they considered "superior." As a matter of fact, these women did not choose to be in the company of these "superiors" in order to protect their strong feelings of self-worth and dignity. This can be related back to our discussion on reference groups, which stated that women who were heads of families identified with other black-women heads of families. Being unable to talk to others for fear of saying "the wrong thing" was not a problem for these women, because "the others," in most instances, were their social support systems. So why be concerned about whether the right thing is being said, when basically, we may be saying the same things—only in different terms? Remember, we share similar experiences. I also asked the 400 black women if they felt that people have to be strong in order to achieve their goals in life. The responses to this question may have various positive implications. The majority of the women either "strongly agreed" or "agreed" that we have to be strong in order to reach our goals. Knowing what we, as black women (whether we are the heads of families or not), are confronted with in everyday life lends support to the idea that we have *emotional* strengths. Determination and perseverance are ways of using our emotional strength in order to cope with unpleasant experiences. Numerous black women I talked to indicated that being on the same level with their support system helped them to establish a good relationship with them. This again brings us back to previous chapters, where the women stated that they identified with other black women in situations similar to their own. "Keeping up with the Joneses" was of little importance to the black-women heads of families. Most of these women did not agree that they tried to live by their friends' standards of living. However, at least 41 percent of the married women stated that they did try to live by their friends' standards of living. When asked if they felt that most of their friends reacted more favorably to them than they reacted to other people, many of the women agreed, again reinforcing the idea that being in situations similar to those of ones' associates helps one to cope better with life experiences. Among both heads of families and nonheads of families, the majority also agreed that "there is not much use in trying hard to please people, because if they are going to like you, they will anyway." With reference to success, the majority of both the heads of families and married women from Mississippi indicated a feeling of success at the time of this research in responding to the following:

> Every person has some idea of what it means to be a success in our society. Do you strongly agree ____, agree ____, disagree ____, strongly disagree ____ that you are a success at present?

However, for the black women who lived in Michigan, more of the married women agreed that they were successful at present than did the heads of families who were unemployed. What accounts for the response difference to this self-esteem item among the two types of women (married and unmarried)? Could it be region or social class? No attempts were made to answer that question in this analysis. In addition, one self-esteem item out of twenty-three does not suggest an inability to cope on the part of the unemployed heads of families from Michigan. As I stated in previous chapters, the black women of both samples told me that they had something available to use in coping with adversity. When asked about chances for reaching their goals in the future, most of the women stated that they felt their chances were "good."

Summarily, my interpretation of what the 400 black women said to me is as follows:

> *"What others see as weaknesses needs to be looked at a little closer to see the strengths that are lying underneath."*

The definition of a "black matriarchy" appears to be a nightmare of our oppressors—not of us, the oppressed. The ability to cope with the stereotypical perceptions about being the heads of families, in addition to adversity in general, means accepting what is real rather than "retreating into fantasy." and that is what we are doing! We are coping!!!

APPENDIX

The items in this Appendix are a part of a larger interview schedule of 176 questions administered to 400 black women in Michigan and Mississippi.

CODE NUMBER _____

1. How many mothers live in this household who are now at home who have been married five years or more, or separated, or are divorced?

_____

2. How old are you? _____

3. What is your marital status?

_____ married

_____ separated

_____ divorced

4. Is this your first marriage?

_____ Yes

_____ No

5. How many children do you have altogether (at home plus away)? _____

6. How many children of your own are living with you?

_____

7. What is the highest grade you completed in school?

_____ Elementary—1, 2, 3, 4, 5, 6

_____ Junior high—7, 8, 9

_____ Senior high—10, 11, 12

_____ College—1, 2, 3, 4

_____ Graduate school: Specify time and degree

_____ Other specialized training for your job—Specify _____

8. How long have you lived in this city? _____

9. What members of this household are employed? (husband, children, niece, nephew, others)?

_____   _____

_____   _____

10. What is the monthly income of each?

_____   _____

_____   _____

11. What kind of work does each one of these people do?

PERSON	*KIND OF WORK*
_____	_____
_____	_____
_____	_____

12. Do you have other sources of income?

_____ Yes

_____ No

13. If yes, what are the other sources of income?

_____

_____

14. Did you live with both natural parents during most of your teenage years?

_____ Yes

_____ No

If no, determine the living environment.

15. If you are employed at present, which one of the following are you?

_____ part-time employed

_____ full-time employed

16. As a working mother, approximately how many hours do you spend away from your children per day?

_____

17. How do you feel about spending time away from your children, even though you have to work to provide for them? Would you say you feel:

_____ very satisfied

_____ somewhat satisfied

_____ somewhat dissatisfied

_____ very dissatisfied

_____ neither satisfied nor dissatisfied

18. When thinking of yourself as a successful or unsuccessful (mother, wife, or provider), with what group of women do you compare yourself?
    (Read whichever of the above words is applicable)

    _____ black women you know

    _____ black women in general

    _____ white women you know

    _____ white women in general

19. When you compare yourself with the other group of women selected above, how would you rank the following as of importance to you? (FOR UNMARRIED WOMEN ONLY)

    _____ being a mother

    _____ being employed

    _____ having lots of friends

20. When you compare yourself with the group of women selected above, how would you rank the following as of importance to you? (FOR MARRIED WOMEN ONLY)

    _____ being a wife

    _____ being a mother

    _____ being employed

    _____ having lots of friends

21. Why do you say that? _____

    _____

    _____

22. In what ways are you successful and/or unsuccessful as a mother? _____

    _____

    _____

23. In what ways are/were you successful and/or unsuccessful as a wife? _____

    _____

    _____

24. Considering your present situation, rank the following groups with which you would like to be compared in the order of importance to you.

    _____ black women who are heads of households

    _____ black women who have husbands

    _____ white women who are heads of households

    _____ white women who have husbands

25. Why did you say that group of women? _____

    _____

    _____

26. Do you strongly agree _____, agree _____, disagree _____, strongly disagree _____ that you are a person of worth as compared with that group of women?

27. Why? _____

28. Do you strongly agree _____, agree _____, disagree _____, strongly disagree _____ that you have number of good qualities as compared to that group of women?

29. Do you strongly agree _____, agree _____, disagree _____, strongly disagree _____ that you are able to do things (in general) as well as that group of women?

30. Do you strongly agree _____, agree _____, disagree _____, strongly disagree _____ that you have much to be proud of as compared with other women?

31. All in all, do you strongly agree _____, agree _____, disagree _____, strongly disagree _____ that you are a failure?

32. Do you strongly agree _____, agree _____, disagree _____, strongly disagree _____ that you sometimes wish that you could have more respect for yourself?

33. On the whole, do you strongly agree _____, agree _____, disagree _____, strongly disagree _____ that you are satisfied with yourself?

34. Do you strongly agree _____, agree _____, disagree _____, strongly disagree _____ that you feel useless at times?

35. Do you strongly agree _____, agree _____, disagree _____, strongly disagree _____ that you are liked by most people?

36. Do you strongly agree _____, agree _____, disagree _____, strongly disagree _____ that in order to get

along and to be liked by people, you try to do what you think they would expect of you?

37. Do you strongly agree _____, agree _____, disagree _____, strongly disagree _____ that you are afraid to let people know what you are really like for fear that they would be disappointed in you?

38. Do you strongly agree _____, agree _____, disagree _____, strongly disagree _____ that when someone says nice things about you, you find it hard to believe that they really mean it?

39. Do you strongly agree _____, agree _____, disagree _____, strongly disagree _____ that you can become so absorbed in your daily activities that it doesn't bother you to not have any intimate friends?

40. Do you strongly agree _____, agree _____, disagree _____, strongly disagree _____ that you worry about what people think of you?

41. Do you strongly agree _____, agree _____, disagree _____, strongly disagree _____ that you feel shy and self-conscious in social situations?

42. Do you strongly agree _____, agree _____, disagree _____, strongly disagree _____ that you feel self-conscious when you are with people whom you think are in a superior position?

43. Do you strongly agree _____, agree _____, disagree _____, strongly disagree _____ that when you are in a group, you are hesitant to talk too much, for fear of saying the wrong thing?

44. Do you strongly agree _____, agree _____, disagree _____, strongly disagree _____ that one must be strong in order to achieve his or her goals in life?

45. Do you strongly agree _____, agree _____, disagree _____, strongly disagree _____ that being on the same level as other people helps you to establish a good relationship with them?

46. Do you strongly agree _____, agree _____, disagree _____, strongly disagree _____ that you try to live by your friends' standard of living?

47. Do you strongly agree _____, agree _____, disagree _____, strongly disagree _____ that most of your friends react more favorably to you than they react to other people?

48. Do you strongly agree _____, agree _____, disagree _____, strongly disagree _____ that there is not much use in trying hard to please people, because if they are going to like you, they will anyway?

49. "Every person has some idea of what it means to be a success in our society." Do you strongly agree _____, agree _____, disagree _____, strongly disagree _____ that you are a success at present?

50. What do you think your chances are in reaching your success goals in the future?

    _____ excellent

    _____ good

_____ fair

_____ poor

51. How many children were in the family that you grew up in? (Include all persons identified as brother and sister related by blood, marriage, or adoption.)

_____

52. Did your father/father substitute ever say it was very important for you to get ahead in life—to make something of yourself by becoming more important and respected by others and obtaining money and the things that money provides? That is: Would you say that he said this:

_____ very often

_____ often

_____ once in a while

_____ seldom or never

53. Do you feel that your father/father substitute actually helped you in getting ahead in life—to make something of yourself? That is: Would you say that he was:

_____ very helpful

_____ helpful

_____ not at all helpful

_____ actually hindered

54. How did your father/father substitute help you in getting ahead in life? PROBE!!! _____

    _____

    _____

    _____

55. How did this man hinder you in getting ahead in life? PROBE!!! _____

    _____

    _____

    _____

56. Did your mother/mother substitute ever say it was very important for you to get ahead in life—to make something of yourself by becoming more important and respected by others and obtaining money and the things that money provides? That is: Would you say that she was:

    _____ very helpful

    _____ helpful

    _____ not at all helpful

    _____ actually hindered

57. Do you feel that your mother/mother substitute actually helped you to get ahead in life—to make something of yourself? That is: Would you say that she was:

    _____ very helpful

    _____ helpful

_____ not at all helpful

_____ actually hindered

58. How did this woman help you in getting ahead in life?
PROBE!!! _____

_____

_____

_____

59. How did this woman hinder you in getting ahead in
life? PROBE!!! _____

_____

_____

_____

60. While you were a teenager, did you feel you wanted to
be like your mother/mother substitute when you grew
up or different from her?

_____ like this woman

_____ different from this woman

(IF DIFFERENT, OMIT 61 AND GO TO 62.)

61. Why did you want to be like this woman? PROBE!!!

_____

_____

_____

62. Why did you want to be different from this woman?
PROBE!!! _____

_____

_____

_____

63. While you were a teenager was there ever anyone like a minister, schoolteacher, a social worker who really took an interest in you and helped you?

_____ Yes (identify) _____

_____ No

64. Do you feel that the Church or religion helped to prepare you for getting ahead in life?

_____ Yes

_____ No

   (IF NO, OMIT 65 AND GO TO 66.)

65. How has the Church or religion helped to prepare you for getting ahead in life? PROBE!!! _____

_____

_____

_____

66. Why do you feel that the Church or religion has not helped to prepare you for getting ahead in life? PROBE!!! _____

_____

_____

_____

67. Who would you say was the *one* woman whom you looked up to and admired more than any other while you were a teenager?

_____ mother/mother substitute

_____ other (identify; i.e. teacher, relative, Sunday School teacher, etc.) _____

68. Companionship has to do with shared leisure or non-work-time activities—e.g. movies, picnics, parties, dancing. Now then, are you generally satisfied _____ or dissatisfied _____ with this aspect of your last marriage?

69. Physical affection (cathectic affection) has to do with feelings and emotions pertaining to the physical aspect of married life. These may range from the most innocent to the most intimate demonstrations of affection. Now then, are you generally satisfied _____ or dissatisfied _____ with this aspect of your last marriage?

70. Do you feel very free _____, free _____, not so free _____ to confide, talk things over, discuss anything with your husband? Or *did* you feel very free _____, free _____, not so free _____ to confide, talk things over, discuss anything with your *last* husband?

71. Do you feel that your husband very readily _____, readily _____, not so readily _____ receives or understands what you are trying to say? Or did you feel that your *last* husband very readily _____, readily _____, not so readily _____ received or understood what you tried to say?

72. How often would you say you and your husband/last ex-husband have/had a big blowup with each other—really get/got angry with each other?

_____ never

_____ seldom

_____ sometimes

_____ often

_____ very often

73. What is/was this usually about?

_____ occupational and financial matters

_____ other (specify) _____

74. Thinking back over your married life, what is the *one* thing that you and your husband/last ex-husband have disagreed about more than others? _____

_____

_____

75. How many sons do you have? _____

76. Is there any particular kind of job that you would like your son(s) to have more than any other?

_____ Yes

_____ No

77. What kind of job do you have in mind for your son(s)?

_____

_____

_____

78. What are the chances that your son(s) will ever have that kind of job?

    _____ excellent

    _____ good

    _____ fair

    _____ poor

79. Are your children's chances of getting ahead much better _____, somewhat better _____, about the same _____ as your chances have been?

80. What is the most important thing for a child to learn to prepare him for life?

    _____ to obey

    _____ to be well-liked and popular

    _____ to think for himself or for herself

    _____ to work hard

    _____ to help others when they need help

81. Does a male companion usually live here with you?

    _____ Yes

    _____ No

BIBLIOGRAPHY

BANKS, JAMES A., and GRAMBS, JEAN. *Black Self-Concept: Implications for Education and the Social Sciences.* New York: McGraw-Hill Book Company, 1972.

BERGER, E. M. "The Relation Between Expressed Acceptance of Self and Expressed Acceptance of Others." *Journal of Abnormal and Social Psychology,* Vol. 47, 1952.

BERNARD, JESSIE. *Marriage and Family Among Negroes.* Englewood Cliffs, N.J.: Prentice-Hall, Inc., 1966.

BILLINGSLEY, ANDREW. *Black Families in White America.* Englewood Cliffs, N.J.: Prentice-Hall, Inc., 1968.

BLUMER, HERBERT. "Sociological Implications of the Thoughts of George Herbert Mead." *American Journal of Sociology,* LXXI, March 1966.

BURGESS, ERNEST W., and LOCKE, HARVEY J. *The Family from Institution to Companionship*. New York: American Book Company, 1945.

CALLUM, MYLES. *Body Talk*. New York: Bantam Books, Inc., 1972.

CLARK, R. E. *Reference Group Theory and Delinquency*. New York: Behavioral Publication, 1972.

DUBOIS, W.E.B. *Darkwaters*. New York: AMS Press, 1969.

ERIKSON, E. H. "The Concept of Identity in Race Relations: Notes and Queries." *Daedalus*. Winter 1966.

FAUNCE, WILLIAM A. "Self-Investment in the Occupational Role." Paper presented at a Meeting of the Southern Sociological Society, New Orleans, April 6, 1972.

FULLERTON, GAIL PUTNEY. *Survival in Marriage: Introduction to Family Interaction, Conflict, and Alternatives*. Hinsdale, Ill.: Dryden Press, 1977.

GORDON, CHAD, and GERGEN, KENNETH J. *The Self in Social Interaction*. New York: John Wiley & Sons, Inc., 1968.

GREEN, ERNEST J. *Personal Relationships: An Approach to Marriage and Family*. New York: McGraw-Hill Book Company, 1978.

GRIER, WILLIAM H., and COBBS, PRICE M. *Black Rage*. New York: Basic Books, Inc., Publishers, 1968.

HENLEY, NANCY M. *"Power, Sex, and Nonverbal Communication."* *Berkeley Journal of Sociology*, Vol. 18, 1974.

HILL, ROBERT B. *The Strengths of Black Families*. New York: Emerson Hall Publishers, Inc., 1971.

JACKSON, JACQUELINE J. "Black Women in a Racist Society," in *Racism and Mental Health*. Edited by Charles C. Willie et al. Pittsburgh, Pa.: University of Pittsburgh Press, 1972.

KARDINER, ABRAM and OVESEY, LIONEL. *The Mark of Oppression: A Psycho-social Study of the American Negro*. New York: W. W. Norton & Co., Inc., 1951.

KARON, BERTRAM. *The Negro Personality.* New York: Springer Publishing Co., Inc., 1958.

LADNER, JOYCE A. *Tomorrow's Tomorrow: The Black Woman.* New York: Doubleday & Company, Inc., 1971.

LAUER, ROBERT H., and HANDEL, WARREN H. *Social Psychology: The Theory and Application of Symbolic Interactionism.* Boston: Houghton Mifflin Company, 1977.

LEWIS, OSCAR. *A Study of Slum Culture.* New York: Random House, Inc., 1968.

MASTERS, WILLIAM H., and JOHNSON, VIRGINIA E. "The Role of Sexual Dysfunction," in *Sexuality and Human Values* edited by Mary S. Calderone. New York: SIECUS/Association Press, 1974.

MEAD, GEORGE HERBERT. *Mind, Self, and Society* edited by Charles W. Morris. Chicago: University of Chicago Press, 1934.

MERTON, ROBERT K. *Social Theory and Social Structure* (Revised and Enlarged Edition). New York: The Free Press, 1957.

MYERS, LENA WRIGHT. "A Study of the Self-Esteem Maintenance Process Among Black Women." Unpublished dissertation, Michigan State University, 1973.

————. "Black Women and Self-Esteem," in *Another Voice: Feminist Perspectives on Social Life and Social Science*, edited by Marcia Millman and Rosabeth Kanter. Garden City, N.Y.: Anchor/Doubleday, 1975.

————. "Black Women: Selectivity Among Roles and Reference Groups in the Maintenance of Self-Esteem." *Journal of Social and Behavioral Sciences*, Vol. 21, Winter 1975.

————. "Mothers from Families of Orientation as Role Models for Black Women." *Northwest Journal of African and Black American Studies*, Vol. 2, Winter 1974.

————. "On Marital Relations: Perceptions of Black Women," in *The Black Woman,* edited by La Frances Rodgers-Rose. Beverly Hills, Calif.: Sage Publications, 1980.

PARSONS, TALCOTT, and CLARK, KENNETH. *The Negro American.* Boston: Beacon Press, 1966.

PETTIGREW, THOMAS F. *A Profile of the Negro American.* Princeton, N.J.: D. Van Nostrand Company, 1964.

POWDERMAKER, HORTENSE. *After Freedom: A Cultural Study in the Deep South.* New York: Viking Press, 1939.

RAINWATER, LEE, and YANCEY, WILLIAM J. *The Moynihan Report and the Politics of Controversy.* Cambridge, Mass. M.I.T. Press, 1967.

REID, INEZ S. *Together Black Women.* New York: Emerson Hall Publishers, Inc., 1972.

REISS, ALBERT. *Occupation and Social Status.* New York: The Free Press, 1961.

ROBINSON, JOHN P., and SHAVER, PHILLIP R. "Measures of Social Psychological Attitudes," Appendix B to *Measures of Political Attitudes.* Ann Arbor, Mich.: Institute for Social Research, The University of Michigan, August 1969.

ROSENBERG, MORRIS. *Society and the Adolescent Self-Image.* Princeton University Press, 1965.

――――. "Psychological Selectivity in Self-Esteem Formation" in *The Self in Social Interaction,* edited by Chad Gordon and Kenneth Gergen. New York: John Wiley & Sons, Inc., 1968.

――――. and SIMMONS, ROBERT G. *Black and White Self-Esteem: The Urban School Child,* Monograph Series. Washington, D.C.: American Sociological Association, July 1971.

SHERWOOD, JOHN J. "Self-Identity and Referent Others." *Sociometry,* Vol. XXVIII, March 1965.

SIMMEL, GEORG. *Conflict and the Web of Group Affiliation,* trans. Kurt H. Wolff. Glencoe, Ill.: The Free Press, 1955.

STAPLES, ROBERT. *The Black Woman in America: Sex, Marriage, and the Family.* Chicago: Nelson Hall Publishers, 1973.

————. "The Myth of the Impotent Black Male." *The Black Scholar*, Vol. 2, 1971.

————. "The Myth of the Black Matriarchy." *The Black Scholar*, Vol. 2, February 1970.

STOTLAND, EZRA, et al. "The Effects of Group Expectations and Self-Esteem Upon Self-Evaluation." *Journal of Abnormal and Social Pyschology*, Vol. LIV, No. 1, January 1957.

U.S. Bureau of the Census. *Census of Housing 1970 Black Statistics Final Report HC (3) 122, Grand Rapids, Michigan, Urbanization Area*. Washington, D.C., 1971.

————. *1970 Census of Population and Housing, Grand Grand Rapids, Michigan*. SMSA, Washington, D.C., 1971.

U.S. Department of Commerce, Bureau of the Census. *Detailed Characteristics of the Population*. Washington, D.C., 1960.

WATKINS, MEL, and DAVID, JAY. *To Be a Black Woman: Portraits in Fact and Fiction*. New York: William Morrow & Co., Inc., 1970.

INDEX

Achievement motivation, 35
Alcohol, 18
Alienation, 35

Banks, James A., 11
Bergen, E. M., 87
Bernard, Jessie, 5
Billingsley, Andrew, 5, 35
Black-female-headed family (*see* Mother-
    headed family)
Black males:
    emasculation myth, 64–67
    employment discrimination, 11
    fathers/father substitutes, 36–38
    relations with wives (*see* Marriage)
    self-image, 11
Blumer, Herbert, 72
Body talk, 72
Broken homes, 9, 12
Burgess, Ernest W., 10, 34

Callum, Myles, 76
Cathetic affection, 73–75, 82
Children:
    discipline of, 13, 82
    as social support systems, 39–40
    (*see also* Mother-headed family)
Child support, 48
Church, 38–39
Clark, Kenneth, 14
Clark, R. E., 21
Cobbs, Price M., 13, 34
College education, 12, 66
Communication, freedom of, 76–77
Companionship, 78–79, 83
Conflict, marital, 79–83
Coping, defined, 5
"Culture of poverty" thesis, 35

Dependence, 12–13, 35
Determination, 89
Disability payments, 48
Discipline, 13, 82
Divorce, 4, 9, 19, 21–22, 74–80, 83
DuBois, W. E. B., 15

Education, 4, 12, 43, 66
Emasculation myth, 64–67
Employment discrimination, 11
Erikson, E. H., 36
Extramarital affairs, 81–82

Family members, as support systems, 34–39
Family stability, 34–35
Fatalistic attitude, 35
Father-child bond, 16
Fathers/father substitutes, 36–38
Faunce, William A., 42
Friends, 20–22, 28, 52, 53, 57

Goals, 89, 91
Grambs, Jean, 11
Grier, William H., 13, 34

Handel, Warren H., 72
Helplessness, 35
Hill, Robert B., 5, 38
Housing, 10

Illegitimacy, 9
Income, 4, 48, 50, 57
Inferiority, 35
Initiative, lack of, 35
Intimate relationships, 71–83

Jackson, Jacqueline J., 5
Johnson, Virginia E., 71

Kardiner, Abram, 11, 12–13, 34
Karon, Bertram P., 9, 10, 34, 35

"Laboring in the field" concept of slavery, 8
Ladner, Joyce A., 5, 73
Lauer, Robert H., 72
Lewis, Oscar, 35
Locke, Harvey J., 10, 34
Love, 70–71

Marriage, 12
    cathetic affection, 73–75, 82
    communication, freedom of, 76–77
    companionship, 78–79, 83
    conflict, 79–83
    nonverbal communication, 74–76, 83
Mass media, 71
Masters, William H., 71
Matriarchy, 8, 91
Mead, George Herbert, 71
Migration, 10
Mother, role of, 23, 43–47, 51–56, 61
Mother-child bond, 10, 35

117

Mother-headed family, 2–3, 14–15
  census data on, 8
  emasculation myth, 64–67
  friends, 20–22
  mothering styles, 12–13
  Moynihan Report on, 9–10
  roles (*see* Roles)
  self-image, 20, 22, 86–91
  slavery and, 10, 35–36
  social support systems (*see* Social support
    systems)
  sons, expectations for, 65–67
Mothers/mother substitutes, as support systems, 28–34
Moynihan, Daniel P., 9–10, 57
*Moynihan Report and the Politics of Con-
  troversy, The* (ed. Rainwater and
  Yancey), 9–10
Myers, L. W., 9
Myth of black emasculation, 64–67

Negro Personality, The (Karon), 35
Nonverbal communication, 74–76, 83
Nonworking wives, 51, 55–57

Ovesey, Lionel, 11, 12–13, 34

Parsons, Talcott, 14
Perseverance, 89
Pettigrew, Thomas, 10–12, 20, 34
Positive aspects of conflict, 80–81
Poverty, 9, 10, 35
Pride, 15
Provider role, 22–23, 44–45, 49–61

Racism, 3, 4, 19
Rainwater, Lee, 9, 14
Recreational facilities, 10
Reid, Inez S., 5
Religion, 38–39
Religious training, 66–67
Renters, 48
Role(s), 23, 42–61
  conflict, 48–61
  expectations, 65–67
  models, 29–34
  selectivity, 44
Rosenberg, Morris, 34, 44, 87

Segregation, 20
Self-Acceptance Scale of 1952, 87
Self-esteem (*see* Self-image)
Self-Esteem Scale of 1965, 87
Self-image, 3, 5, 11, 15, 20, 22, 86–91
Self-pity, 19
Separation, 4, 9, 19, 45, 74, 76–80, 83
Sexism, 3, 4, 19
Sexuality, 36, 70–75, 82
Shyness, 88
Simmel, Georg, 80
Slavery, 8, 10, 35–36
Social interaction, 71–83
Socialization, 72
Social Security, 48
Social situations, comfort in, 88–89
Social support systems, 26–40, 87
  children, 39–40
  church and religion, 38–39
  defined, 26
  family members, 34–39
  fathers/father substitutes, 36–38
  friends, 20–22, 28, 52, 53, 57
  mothers/mother substitutes, 28–34
Sons, expectations for, 65–67
Spouse battering, 81
Standards of living, 89–90
Staples, Robert, 5, 22, 64
Success, 90
Symbolic interaction, 72, 73

Tranquilizers, 19

Unconscious (nonsignificant) social interaction, 72
Unemployment, 10–11

Verbal communication, 76–77

Welfare system, 58
Widowhood, 4, 19
Wife, role of, 51–56, 61
Working women, 22–23, 44–45, 49–61

Yancey, William J., 9